Pupil's Book 2

ICT InteraCT
for KS3

Pupil's Book **2**

ICT InteraCT
for KS3

Bob Reeves
Consultant: Alan Plumpton

DL **DYNAMIC LEARNING**

HODDER EDUCATION
AN HACHETTE UK COMPANY

The Publishers would like to thank the following for permission to reproduce copyright material:

Photo credits: p.5 *t* © Patrick Eden/Alamy, *b* Kindra Clineff/Index Stock Imagery/photolibrary.com;
p.8 © Corbis; **p.11** *t* © Marianna Day Massey/Zuma/Corbis, *b* © Lili K./Zefa/Corbis; **p.19 and 21**
© David Trevor/Alamy; **p.22** Mehdi Fedouach/AFP/Getty Images; **p.24** © Sean Justice/Corbis; **p.25** © Alan
Schein Photography/Corbis; **p.27** *l* Henry Horenstein/Stone/Getty Images, *c* © Kevin Dodge/Corbis, *r* Tom
Schierlitz/Stone/Getty Images; **p.51** © Charles Gullung/Zefa/Corbis; **p.60** © Paul Rapson/Alamy; **p.62** © Martin
Williams/Alamy; **p.74** © Adrian Sherratt/Alamy; **p.81** © Andrew Howe/iStockphoto.com; **p.82** © Kevin
Foy/Alamy; **p.86** © Tim Graham/Alamy; **p.88** © Stock Connection Blue/Alamy; **p.93** © Pete Saloutos/Corbis;
p.94 © David Woods/Corbis; **p.95** © Manor Photography/Alamy; **p.104** © Alan Oliver/Alamy; **p.107** ©
Blackred/iStockphoto.com; **p.108** *t* Massimo Rossi/Photononstop/ Photolibrary.com, *b* © Dominic Harris/Alamy;
p.109 *t* © Ian Shaw/Alamy, *b* © Vario images GmbH & Co.KG/Alamy; **p.111** *t* NASA/ Science Photo Library, *l* ©
Photodisc/Alamy, *b* Jim Reed/Science Photo Library; **p.116** Martin Bond/Science Photo Library; **p.117** © Crown
copyright 2007, the Met Office.

Acknowledgements: p.10, **15** and **98** Google; **p.11** The FA.com; **p.12** *t* and **31** BBC.co.uk;
p.12 *b* www.realbuzz.com; **p.17** Altavista.com; **p.20** Natural History Museum; **p.29** and **41** www.lifebytes.gov.uk;
p.30 YouTube; **p.45** Tiscali; **p.58** The Sims; **p.59** Microsoft; **p.71** Match.com; **p.92** © Miguel Angel/
iStockphoto.com; **p.100** © Jason Carreiro/iStockphoto.com; **p.101** © Joaquin Croxatto/iStockphoto.com;
p.115 Choose and Book system, NHS website.

Screenshots reprinted by permission of Microsoft Corporation, Microsoft and Windows are trademarks of
Microsoft Corporation.

t=top, *b*=bottom, *l*=left, *r*=right

Every effort has been made to trace all copyright holders, but if any have been inadvertently overlooked the
Publishers will be pleased to make the necessary arrangements at the first opportunity.

Although every effort has been made to ensure that website addresses are correct at time of going to press,
Hodder Education cannot be held responsible for the content of any website mentioned in this book. It is
sometimes possible to find a relocated web page by typing in the address of the home page for a website in the
URL window of your browser.

Hachette UK's policy is to use papers that are natural, renewable and recyclable products and made from wood
grown in well-managed forests and other controlled sources. The logging and manufacturing processes are expected to
conform to the environmental regulations of the country of origin.

Orders: please contact Hachette UK Distribution, Hely Hutchinson Centre, Milton Road, Didcot, Oxfordshire, OX11 7HH.
Telephone: +44 (0) 1235 827827. Email education@hachette.co.uk Lines are open from 9 a.m. to 5 p.m., Monday to Friday.
You can also order through our website: www.hoddereducation.co.uk

© Bob Reeves 2008
First published in 2008 by
Hodder Education,
an Hachette UK Company
Carmelite House, 50 Victoria Embankment
London, EC4Y 0DZ

Impression number   19
Year   2022

Cover photo Jupiter Images/Corbis
Illustrations by Richard Duszczak, Tony Jones/Art Construction
Case Study introduction artworks by Magic Software Pvt. Ltd.
Typeset in 13.5/15pt ITC Officina Sans by Stephen Rowling/Springworks
Produced by DZS Grafik, Printed in Bosnia & Herzegovina

A catalogue record for this title is available from the British Library

ISBN: 978 0340 940 983

CONTENTS

Introduction   2

Module 1   Finding and presenting information   4

Module 2   Web design and creation   24

Module 3   Modelling   46

Module 4   Data handling   64

Module 5   Control   80

Module 6   Wider aspects of ICT   96

Module 7   Integrated tasks   110

Keywords Glossary   118

Index   124

INTRODUCTION

Welcome to ICT InteraCT Book 2. The book has seven main *modules*:

> Module 1 Finding and presenting information
> Module 2 Web design and creation
> Module 3 Modelling
> Module 4 Data handling
> Module 5 Control
> Module 6 Wider aspects of ICT
> Module 7 Integrated tasks

Each of these modules has several *units*. The book is designed so that every unit takes up either two or four pages of the book. There are 30 units in total, which sounds a lot, but the course is designed to be flexible and your teacher will tell you what they'd like you to cover!

There is a website to support this course, which contains an electronic copy of the book and lots of other resources that you'll need to boost your knowledge and understanding of ICT, and to develop your practical skills. Your teacher will show you the electronic version of the book and you will find that its layout looks exactly the same as the printed pages. The electronic version works a bit like a web page because it has lots of links in it that will open up other resources.

You will notice that all the pages have various icons on them. On the electronic version of the book, these icons will link you to the other resources. Before you get started, it is worth having a quick look at how the pages are laid out and what each of the icons mean.

Here is a list of the icons you will come across in this book:

 Written Tasks

 Practical Tasks

 Skills Tutorials

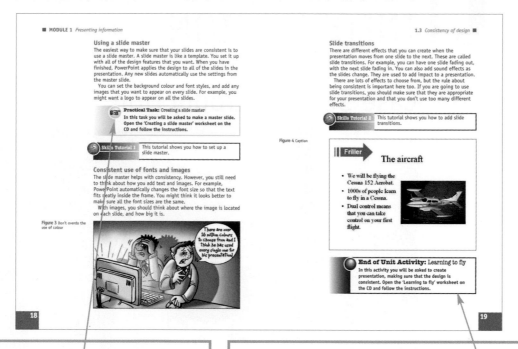

 Skills Tutorials: These are 'how to' guides that will show you how to do things on the computer.

Practical Tasks: These are small tasks where you will be asked to do something on the computer.

End of Unit Activities: These are larger tasks where you can show how well you have understood what you have learnt during the unit.

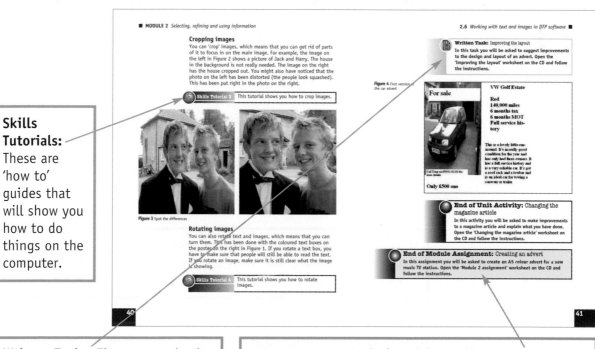

 Written Tasks: These are tasks that you don't need a computer for. Your teacher might ask you to do these for homework, or you might do them if you have a lesson when you are not in the computer room.

  End of Module Assignments: These are mini-projects that might take a lesson or more to complete. There is one at the end of every module. You can show how well you have understood what you have learnt in the module.

Case Study introduction

Figure 1 Arthur in the Visitor Centre

This is Arthur. He is the Tourism Officer for the Leak District National Park. The National Park is one of the largest in the country and is very popular with walkers, horse-riders, cyclists and day-trippers who visit the local towns and tourist attractions. Arthur works here at the Visitor Centre. Around one million people a year visit the Leak District and many of them come to the Visitor Centre to get information about the area. It is Arthur's job to make sure that people can get access to this information and that the information is accurate and up to date.

> **Q** What information might people want to know? Where can Arthur get the information from? How can he be sure that the information is reliable and accurate?

Arthur collects together lots of different information. Some of the information is about the history of the local area, including sites of interest. He also collects information about activities that people might like to take part in. There are lots of shops, hotels and restaurants in the local area that advertise through the Visitor Centre. Arthur uses the Internet to find out some of the information he needs.

Figure 2 Arthur in his office

> **Q** What search engines could Arthur use? Why would he use one search engine rather than another?

Figure 3 shows a typical web page that Arthur might look at when he is doing his research. It is for one of several hotels in the local area. It contains information about the hotel and how to contact it. The hotel has asked Arthur if he can include a hyperlink to the hotel website from the Leak District National Park website.

Figure 3 Website for Paulin's Hotel

> **Q** Can Arthur trust the information that is on the Paulin Hotel website? Why might the information on the hotel website be biased? Is the information on the website based on fact or opinion?

Arthur loves the Leak District. It has a long and interesting history. It has some very interesting places of interest. For example, Pam's Peak is the highest point in the Leak District at 650 metres above sea level. On a clear day, you can see for 30 miles. Rocky Crag is a 200-metre-high rock formation, which is very popular with climbers. There are about a dozen places of local interest like this. One of Arthur's jobs is to provide people with information about these places.

> **Q** In what different ways could Arthur present the information to the tourists?

Figure 4 Multimedia consoles in the Visitor Centre

The Visitor Centre has a number of information consoles where visitors can view multimedia presentations about the local area. Each console consists of a touch screen display and a speaker. Arthur has put together a slideshow, which gives details on places of local interest. The slideshow is quite long with about 25 slides in total. It runs on a loop, so that when it has finished it starts all over again.

Q What problems might there be with the way that Arthur has set up the slideshow? How could he make the slideshow more suitable for the audience?

Arthur has worked at the Visitor Centre for many years and over that time he has extended the range of information he gives to visitors. For example, the slideshows are popular but one of the problems with them is that you can only view them in the Visitor Centre. When visitors are out and about in the Leak District National Park, they need information with them.

Q What different types of information do the visitors need? What is the best way of providing this information in each case?

Figure 5 Information stands in the Visitor Centre

1.1 | Evaluating information found on websites

In this unit you will learn:
> **Techniques for evaluating information on websites**
> **How to work out whether a website is reliable**
> **How to tell the difference between a fact and an opinion**

Websites

Website ownership

There is so much information available on the Internet, that it is not always easy to tell whether we can trust the information that we find. There are several techniques that you can use to test whether you think information is reliable or not.

The first thing you should do is check the website address, also known as a URL. There are some clues that will help you to find out where the information has come from and what kind of organisation or person is behind the website. For example:

.gov.uk	This means that the website is owned by the UK government.
.org	This means that the website is owned by a charity or other organisation (but not a business).
.com or .co.uk	This means that the website is owned by a company or business.
.sch	This means that the website is owned by a UK school.
.ac	This means that the website is owned by a college or university.
.uk	This is the country code and shows which country the website owner is operating from. There are lots of these, e.g. au, it, de, ch.
.tv	This means that the website probably has a lot of multimedia content and is used to broadcast information.

You should think about what type of person or organisation owns the website and what their purpose might be in having the website.

Trusting the information

Understanding the URL is a good start, but it still doesn't tell you everything. For example, there are millions of websites that end in .co.uk or .com and many of these may be unreliable.

Another check you can do is to find out more about the person or organisation behind the website. You should always ask yourself why they are putting the information onto a website, for example:

Written Task:
Trusting websites

In this task you will be asked to think about why information appears on websites. Open the 'Trusting websites' worksheet on the website and follow the instructions.

> www.dcsf.gov.uk is the Department for Children, Schools and Families. They are the part of the government responsible for education. Therefore, most of the information has been put there to *inform* pupils, teachers and parents.
> www.tesco.com is the website of the well-known supermarket chain. They put information on the website to *inform* us of what they are selling and to *persuade* us to buy things.
> www.youtube.com is a website where people can post video clips to *entertain* and *inform*.

You can also look at the links from the website. For example, if there is lots of advertising on the site and you get lots of pop-ups, then you are likely to be on a commercial site where they are trying to sell you something. If there are links to well-known organisations like government websites or charities, then you can probably trust the information more.

Facts and opinions

Whenever you read information from websites, you should always think about whether the information is a **fact** or an **opinion**. For example:

> 'Sales of song downloads have overtaken those of traditional CDs.' Source: BBC.
> This is a fact. It has come from a reliable source and it can be checked using other sources.
> 'I think that in 5 years' time it will be impossible to buy CDs – it will all be done by downloads.' Source: Music download site.
> This is an opinion. It is what one person thinks and we cannot check the information. Also, we don't know who they are and what they are basing the statement on.

End of Unit Activity: Evaluating information

In this activity, you will be asked to evaluate information found on websites. Open the 'Evaluating information' worksheet on the website and follow the instructions.

1.2 | Checking the validity of information

In this unit you will learn:
> **How to assess whether information is valid**
> **To look at where the information comes from**
> **To look for bias**
> **To look at how up-to-date information is**

Introduction

In Unit 1.1 we looked at whether we could trust information or not by looking at who owned the website and why they put the information on the Internet. In this unit, we look at further techniques you can use to decide whether information is valid or not.

Checking validity

If information is valid, this means that it is true. Sometimes it can be difficult to tell what is true and what isn't. For example, if you wanted to find out the most popular sport in the UK, an Internet search will show you that:

> 'Football is the most popular sport in the UK.'
> 'Fishing is the most popular sport in the UK.'

So which of these two 'facts' is true?

Figure 1 Using a search engine

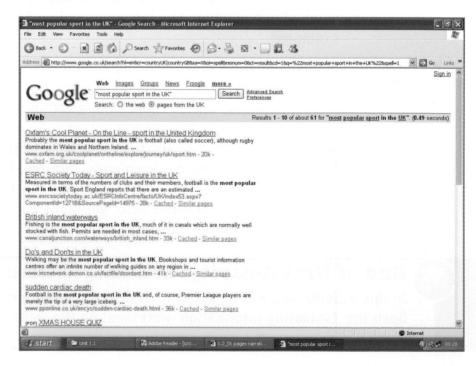

One way to find out is to look at the hits you get back from a search engine and to look at the links to see where they come from. For example, a Google search for 'most popular sport in the UK' will show links that say it is football and links that say it is fishing. By reading the descriptions listed in the search engine, you will see that these links are to:

> websites run by local football clubs and local fishing clubs
> online articles from well-known newspapers
> government research websites
> forums and chat rooms about football or fishing.

Some of these sites say it is football, some say it is fishing, so we still don't know. We could probably trust the information from the newspapers and the Government more than we could from the clubs or chat rooms.

If you can't work out who is behind a website, go to the home page, or the About Us page to see if you can find out who they are and why they have a website. If that doesn't help then look at whether there are links from the site to other sites that you have heard of. If there are links to well-known sites, you may trust this site more. If all the links are advertising you might just think that they are trying to sell you something.

 Written Task: Checking validity

In this task you will be asked to check the validity of information found on websites. Open the 'Checking validity' worksheet on the website and follow the instructions.

Figure 2 The About Us page from the Football Association website

Bias

Another thing to look at is whether there is likely to be any bias in the information. For example, some websites might have a particular interest in saying one thing or another.

In this case, the websites of the local clubs, forums and chat rooms may not be reliable as the information is given by people who love their particular sport. It's a bit like arguing with a friend over which is the best band on the planet or what is the best programme on television.

Figure 3 These two websites disagree about which is the most popular sport

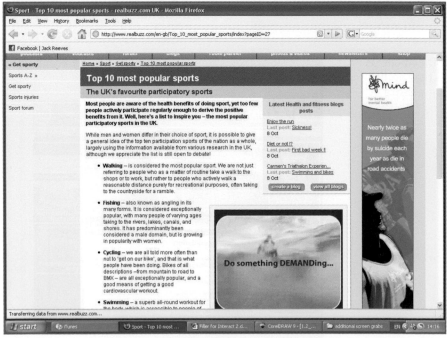

The information may be biased because the website is trying to persuade you to have a certain opinion, or maybe it is just trying to sell you something. For example, one of the sites that says fishing is most popular is a travel business that arranges fishing trips.

Up-to-date information

Another check is to see how up-to-date the information is. The most popular sport in the UK this year might not be the same as last year. Information can change quickly. For example, if you were trying to find the cheapest flight to Spain, that could be changing every minute.

Some information does not change and this makes it easier to check. For example, if you were asked to find out when Henry VIII was king or who invented the light bulb, then these facts do not change over time.

Figure 4 Which is more popular – football or fishing?

 End of Unit Activity: Football or fishing – you decide

In this activity, you will be asked to evaluate whether information found on websites is valid or biased. Open the 'Football of fishing – you decide' worksheet on the website and follow the instructions.

1.3 Choosing a search engine

Learning Objectives	In this unit you will learn:
	> **How to choose which search engine to use**
	> **How search engines work**
	> **How results are ranked**
	> **How the results at the top might not be the most relevant**

Introduction

Most people have a favourite search engine that they use every time they need to find something on the Internet. For example, Google is popular at the moment and millions of people use it every day. There are actually hundreds of different search engines to choose from and you might find that some of them are better than others depending on what you are searching for.

Why are there so many search engines? The main reason is that there is so much information on the Internet that one search engine can't look through all of it. No one really knows how many web pages there are on the Internet but some estimate it at around 12 billion – that's 12,000,000,000! Another problem is that the information on these pages is changing all the time.

Practical Task: Search engines

In this task you will be asked to think about which search engine you use and why. Open the 'Search engines' worksheet on the website and follow the instructions.

Figure 1 Some popular search engines

Figure 2 Selecting a search engine

How search engines work

Most search engines work in the same way – you type in the keywords and the search engine lists all the results, which are usually called 'hits'. You then click on a link from the results page and it takes you to that website.

The search engine has to work out which sites to include in the results and which order to put them in. A site is included in the results if it contains the same keywords as the ones you typed into the search engine. This is why if you type something general like 'shop' you get millions of hits: the word 'shop' is on millions of web pages.

Figure 3 A Google search for shops showing millions of hits

The search engine then has to work out how to rank the results. It does this by working out which website is most relevant to your keywords. It looks at the web pages listed in the results page and then counts how many links these web pages have to other web pages with the same keywords in.

For example, if we do a search for 'concert tickets', the search engine lists every web page that has those two words next to each other in the web page. There will be thousands (see Figure 4).

Figure 4 Deciding which website is relevant

Keywords	Results	Number of links	Ranking
	Web page 1	5200	2
	Web page 2	8400	1
"concert tickets"	Web page 3	2300	3
	Web page 4	1200	4

The 'Number of links' column in Figure 4 shows how many other web pages are linked to each result. In this case, web page 2 has got the highest number of links, which means that the search engine would put web page 2 at the top of the results page.

> **Written Task:** Keywords
>
> **In this task you will be asked to work out what keywords to type into a search engine. Open the 'Keywords' worksheet on the website and follow the instructions.**

Sponsored links

One thing to watch out for is what are called **sponsored links**. The Internet has millions of web pages where the main purpose is to sell you something. The people that run these web pages can pay the search engines to make sure that their site is listed near the top of the results.

In some search engines you can see which are the sponsored links. For example, in AltaVista, a search for 'mp3 players' brings up sponsored links at the top of the search and down the right-hand side (see Figure 5).

Figure 5 Some links are sponsored

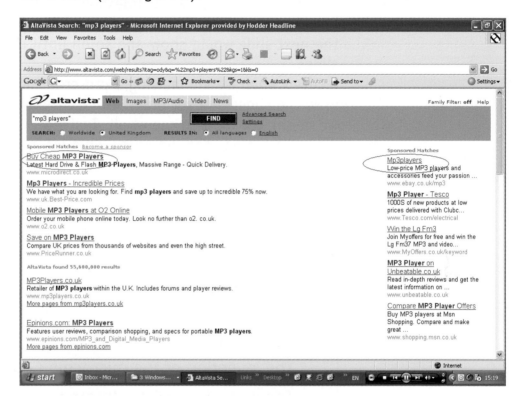

Sponsored links can be useful and help you find what you want more quickly. However, you need to be aware of them because you might click on the first result in the list thinking that it is the most relevant. This might not be true as it might be at the top because the owner of the web page has paid for it to be at the top.

 End of Unit Activity: Group research

In this activity you will work in a group to find information on the Internet using a search engine. Open the 'Group research' worksheet on the website and follow the instructions.

1.4 | Presenting information using a slideshow

Learning Objectives

In this unit you will learn how to:
> **Add hyperlinks to a slideshow**
> **Create an interactive presentation**

Introduction

In InteraCT 1, we created slideshow presentations using PowerPoint. We set them up so that when you clicked the mouse, the next slide would show and so on until there were no more slides.

Often when we are viewing a presentation, we don't want to view the slides in a set order. In fact there are some slides that we might not want to see at all. Instead, we want to click on different options depending on what we are interested in.

Figure 1 A slide with links

The history of computers

Click on the links below to find out more:

The war years (1939-45)

The invention of the microchip (1960s)

The early days of the Internet (1960s)

The first PCs (1980s)

The invention of the World Wide Web (1980s)

Computing today (2000 onwards)

Written Task: Planning a slideshow

In this task you will be asked to plan a slideshow that includes hyperlinks. Open the 'Planning a slideshow' worksheet on the website and follow the instructions.

Figure 1 shows the opening slide of a slideshow about the history of computers. The standard way to show this presentation would be to show the audience all the slides one after another.

If someone was really interested in the Computing today (2000 onwards) section, but not interested in anything else, they would have to click through many slides to get to the interesting bit.

The solution to this is to add hyperlinks to the slideshow so that the person watching it can go directly to the slides they are interested in.

Figure 2 An interactive presentation in a museum

 **Skills Tutorial 1** | This tutorial shows you how to create a hyperlink in PowerPoint.

Adding hyperlinks

You are already used to using hyperlinks as they are used a lot on web pages. A hyperlink is something (text or an image) that you click on to take you to another page. You can add hyperlinks in many different programs. For example, you can add hyperlinks:

> in a word processor to link different pages on a document
> to a spreadsheet to link to different worksheets
> in a slideshow to link to different slides.

 Practical Task: Adding hyperlinks

In this task you will be asked to add hyperlinks to a slideshow. Open the 'Adding hyperlinks' worksheet on the website and follow the instructions.

You have to think carefully about your links. You need to decide:

> Do you put the link on a piece of text, or on a picture, or both?
> After a link has been clicked, do you have a link from the new slide back to the original slide?
> How can the person using the slideshow keep track of where they are once they have clicked on a few links?

Some slideshows have a list of options on every slide so that the person using it always knows where they are. This technique is used a lot on websites too. In the example from the Natural History Museum in Figure 3, the menu bar is near the top of every page of the website.

Figure 3 A standard menu bar on a web page

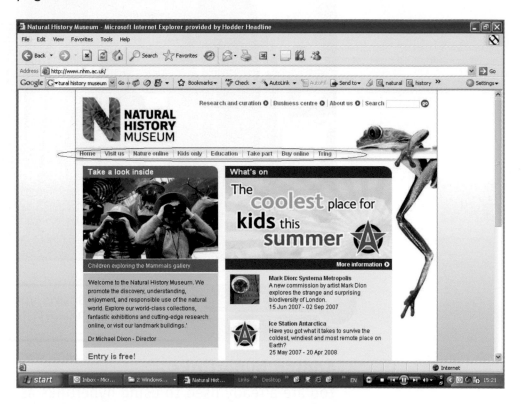

Creating an interactive presentation

The use of hyperlinks makes a presentation much more interactive. This means that the person viewing the slideshow is able to have much more control over which bits they want to see.

Interactive slideshows are useful in lots of different situations. For example, when you go to a museum, they have interactive slideshows on computer consoles that let you find out more about the exhibits.

Figure 4 Using an interactive slideshow

There are some situations where an interactive display would not be suitable. For example, if the slideshow were being used as part of a presentation to a large group, the presenter would need to click through the slides in the order that fits their speech.

 End of Unit Activity: Creating an interactive slideshow

In this activity you will be asked to create an interactive slideshow. Open the 'Creating an interactive slideshow' worksheet on the website and follow the instructions.

Figure 5 Using hyperlinks

1.5 Presenting information using audio

In this unit you will learn how to:
> **Gather information for a news report**
> **Select the relevant information for the report**
> **Plan and write a script for the report**
> **Make a sound recording**

Audio

News reporting

The purpose of this unit is to plan and then record a one-minute-long radio news report. When the news is reported it is important to present an unbiased view of the topic. This means that you should include different points of view.

Most news reports try to be balanced, but sometimes they can be biased. For example, listen to the two radio news reports on the website, which are all about plans to build incinerators to burn rubbish in the UK.

> **Written Task:** News reports
>
> **In this task you will be asked to compare two different news reports. Open the 'News reports' worksheet on the website and follow the instructions.**

Figure 1 News reporter

Gathering information

News reporters gather information from lots of different sources. They use many of the same sources that we use, such as the Internet. They also carry out interviews with people. In the case of the incinerators, they might collect the following information from the following people:

> local people – to find out what effect they think it will have on their lives
> the company who run the incinerator – to find out how much rubbish they will be burning and how much pollution it creates
> environmental campaigners – to find out what the environmental damage might be
> the local council – to find out how many jobs it might create, or how else they could get rid of the rubbish.

This is a good example of a topic where people might have different views about the same thing.

Figure 2 Audio information reaches many people

Planning your news report

Creating a radio news article is different from the ways in which you have presented information so far using ICT. The main differences are:

> you can only use words and sounds – no pictures
> you have to fill an exact amount of time, e.g. one minute.

This makes planning important as you must make your report interesting to listen to and include all the information in a short space of time. A suitable plan might be:

> Collect information from different sources.
> Decide on the key points you want to make. Make sure that you cover all sides of the argument.
> Write a first draft of the script summarising all the information you have collected.
> Read the script to check timings.
> Edit the script to make sure it is one minute long.
> Record the script.

Recording the report

Once your script is ready to read, you can record it. You will need a microphone of some sort and some sound recording software. There is a basic sound recorder option in Windows.

There is also specialist software with extra features, such as being able to edit the sound after you have recorded it. One example is Audacity, which is available as a free download from the Internet.

Skills Tutorial 1

This tutorial shows you how to use the Windows sound recorder.

Skills Tutorial 2

This tutorial shows you how to record sounds using Audacity.

End of Unit Activity: Radio news article

In this activity you will be asked to create and record your own radio news report. Open the 'Radio news article' worksheet on the website and follow the instructions.

End of Module Assignment: Creating a presentation

In this assignment you will be asked to create a multimedia presentation for a local tourist attraction. You will have to adapt the presentation to make it suitable for people who are visually impaired. Open the 'Module 1 assignment' worksheet on the website and follow the instructions.

21 WEB DESIGN AND CREATION

························ ## Case Study introduction

Figure 1 Zoe Chan

This is Zoe Chan. She's a web designer. She's been asked by a company called Popper Party Planners to redesign their website: www.popperpartyplanners.com. Before we look at their website, let's take a look at what they do. Popper Party Planners have been in business for around a year. They are an online business and you can use their website to organise everything you might need for a party, however big or small. They specialise in 18th and 21st birthday parties and school and college balls. For example, you can hire a stretched limousine or party clothes, book a band or a DJ, or hire a venue.

> **Q** What is the purpose of their website? Who is the audience for their website?

Now let's take a look at the website.

Figure 2 Home page of Popper Party Planners

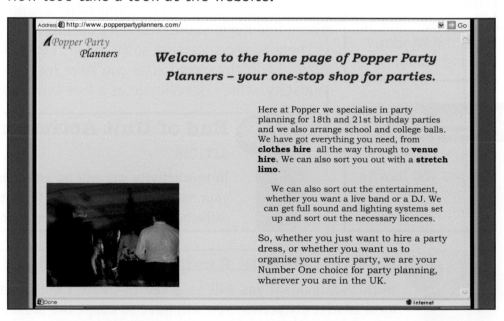

This is the home page. Zoe clicks on a link to the page on stretch limos.

Figure 3 Stretch limos page

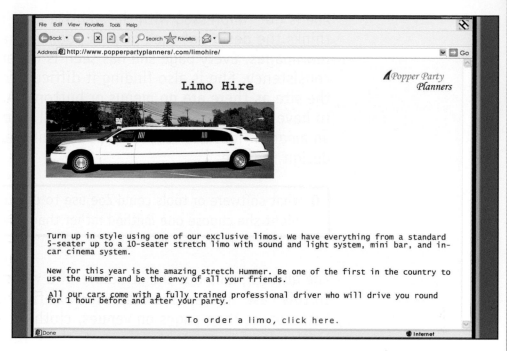

Zoe decides to look at some more of the web pages to see if they are any better. She clicks on the link to the clothes hire page. She notices that this page looks different from the two she has already looked at. She reads this one in a bit more detail.

Figure 4 Clothes hire page

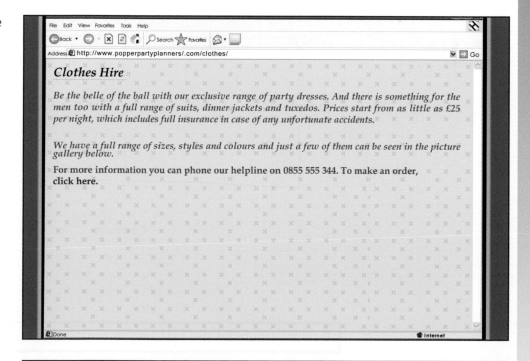

Q What do you like about the design of these pages? What problems might there be with the design of these two pages? How clear is the information on the page? Does it give you all the information you need?

Zoe is not impressed with the website as it is at the moment. She thinks the design of each page is poor as there is lots of text and few images. Every page she has seen is different and there is no consistency. She is also finding it difficult to find her way round the site as there are no menus or buttons. All the hyperlinks seem to have been put on randomly. All in all, she thinks it is a bit of an amateur job! Zoe realises that she will need to completely re-design the site.

> **Q** What software or tools could Zoe use to create the website? Why might she choose one method rather than another?

Zoe always plans out the structure of a website before she starts. In this case she realises that there are five main pages. There is a home page, then pages on venues, clothing and limos and then the booking page. At the moment, there is no structure to the way that the pages are linked together. She decides that it needs a clear structure. She draws out a diagram of how she wants it to link together.

Figure 5 Zoe's new website design

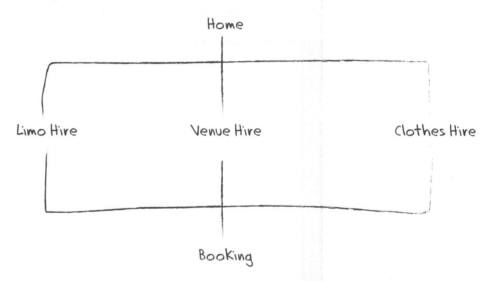

> **Q** What would be the best way to create the links on each page?

Zoe has started working on the design of the web page. Once she is happy with this she plans to use it as a template for all the other pages. She has re-designed the home page and the clothes hire page to start with.

Q In what ways is Zoe's new design an improvement on the original web pages?

Figure 6 Zoe's new home page

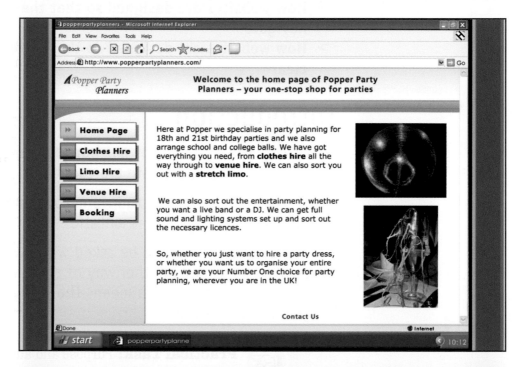

Figure 7 Zoe's new clothes hire page

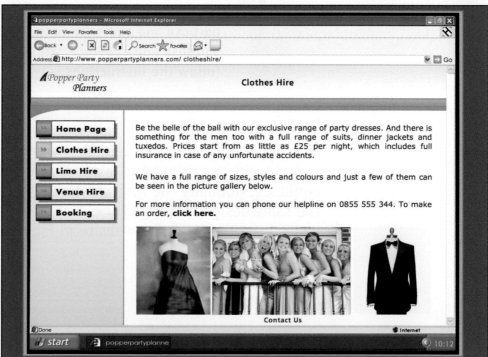

2.1 Reviewing web page design

Introduction

We already know how important **purpose** and **audience** are in ICT. For example, when we create a presentation, we have to consider:

> Purpose – are we trying to inform, persuade or entertain?
> Audience – who is the presentation for?

The same questions should be asked when we are designing web pages. Web pages are another way of presenting information. They are multimedia, which means that they can consist of text, images, video and sound.

 Practical Task: Purpose and audience

In this task you will be asked to think about the purpose and audience for a website. Open the 'Purpose and audience' worksheet on the website and follow the instructions.

Web page design

Web pages are the individual pages that make up a website. The website will be designed in a way that is appropriate for the audience. Normally the individual pages of a website will share the same design features. For example, take a look at the two web pages from the LifeBytes website in Figure 1.

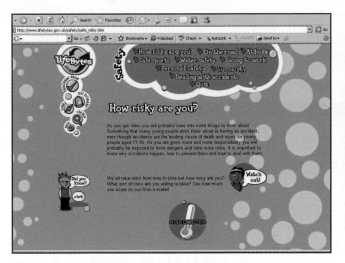 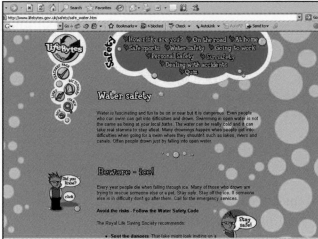

Figure 1 The LifeBytes website has a consistent design

Notice how similar the two pages look. They both have:

> the same orange and yellow background
> the LifeBytes logo in the same place
> the list of links in the same place in the top right corner
> the name of the page centred at the top
> a balance of graphics and text
> the same style of graphics.

 Written Task: Web page design

In this task you will be asked to think about how web pages are designed to appeal to certain people. Open the 'Web page design' worksheet on the website and follow the instructions.

Navigation

Websites can get big. For example, the BBC website has hundreds of thousands of pages. This can be a problem as people using the site may find it difficult to find their way around and get the information they are looking for.

Moving around a website is known as **navigating**. Later in this module you will create a website and you need to think carefully about how people will be able to navigate around your site.

Look at the example in Figure 2, which is from YouTube. YouTube contains thousands of videos posted by individuals all over the world. All the web pages are designed in a certain way to make navigation easier.

Figure 2 Navigation features of YouTube

Tabs are used for their four main categories.

Links are listed down the left-hand side.

There are thumbnail images and links to the most viewed videos.

The Search box is always in the centre under the tabs.

The Upload Videos link is always in this position on every page.

There are adverts down the right-hand side.

Clarity of information

Clarity refers to whether or not information is clear and easy to understand. When you are creating web pages, you must make sure that the information is clear. How you do this depends on the purpose and audience. For example:

> The YouTube website is clear as it only uses a small amount of text to explain what each video is.
> The LifeBytes website is also clear as it does not use any unnecessary text and the text it does use for links is always in a large font and in bold.

Compare Figures 1 and 2 with the main BBC news page in Figure 3; it is less clear as there is much more text and lots of links all over the page.

Figure 3 Is the BBC news site clear enough?

However, this page has to show much more information and it is for an older audience that is willing to take some time to read the information carefully.

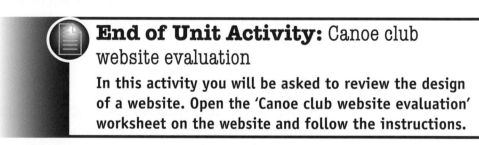

End of Unit Activity: Canoe club website evaluation

In this activity you will be asked to review the design of a website. Open the 'Canoe club website evaluation' worksheet on the website and follow the instructions.

Figure 4 Information is not always as clear as it could be

2.2 | Methods for creating web pages

In this unit you will learn:
> How HTML is used to create a basic web page
> How Microsoft Word and Microsoft Publisher can be used to create web pages
> How specialised software can be used to create web pages
> How to select the most appropriate software for creating web pages

Introduction

There are several different ways that you can create web pages. The three main options are:

> Use a 'mark-up language' such as HTML: to do this you have to learn to write in a special code that tells your web browser how to display the information on the page.
> Use Microsoft Word or Microsoft Publisher: there are options in both programs that allow you to create web pages.
> Use specialist software such as Microsoft FrontPage or Adobe Dreamweaver: this software is designed specifically to create web pages.

HTML

HTML stands for Hypertext Markup Language. It is code that contains instructions that describe how a web page is displayed on screen. The easiest way to understand it is to look at some HTML code examples. Figure 1 shows the beginning of a simple web page in a browser. Figure 2 shows the HTML code used to create it.

Figure 1 Example web page

Figure 2 The HTML code that is used for Figure 1

```
HTML.txt - Notepad
File   Edit   Format   View   Help

<HTML>
<Head>
<Title> Basic HTML example </title>
</head>

<body bgcolor = "yellow">

<font face = "Arial" align = "centre" size = 10>
<p> welcome to the page
</font>
<br>

<font face = "Times" size = 4>
<p> This is an example of some html code
<br> It has been written using a <b> Notepad </b> </p>

</font>
</body>
</HTML>|
```

Each line of HTML code tells the browser what to display on the page and how to display it. For example:

Code	Result
`<body bgcolor="yellow">`	Tells the browser to set the background colour to yellow
`<font face="Times" size=4>`	Tells the browser to set the font style to Times at font size 4.
`<p>This is an example of some html code   It has been written using a <b> Notepad </b> </p>`	The `<p>` shows the start of a paragraph and the `</p>` shows the end. The ` ` shows a break of line. This code makes the two lines of text appear on the screen.

Written Task: HTML

In this task you will be asked to work out some HTML code. Open the 'HTML' worksheet on the website and follow the instructions.

Using standard software to create web pages

HTML can get complicated, as you have to know how to write the code in the correct way. This is why many people create websites using software. For example, web pages can be created using Microsoft Word or Microsoft Publisher. You use the software in the normal way and then use 'save as' to save the page in HTML format. Microsoft Word or Microsoft Publisher then writes the HTML code for you.

 Practical Task: Comparing methods

In this task you will be asked to compare two different ways of creating web pages. Open the 'Comparing methods' worksheet on the website and follow the instructions.

 **Skills Tutorial 1**   This tutorial shows you how to use Microsoft Word to create a web page.

 **Skills Tutorial 2**   This tutorial shows you how to use Microsoft Publisher to create a web page.

Using specialised software to create web pages

There are also lots of specialised programs that can be used to create web pages. For example, many professional website designers use a program called Adobe Dreamweaver. Another option is Microsoft FrontPage, which usually comes as part of Microsoft Office.

Both of these programs have special features that are designed to help you create more advanced websites than you can in Microsoft Word or Microsoft Publisher.

 **Skills Tutorial 3**   This tutorial shows you how to use Microsoft FrontPage to create a web page.

Choosing which software to use

This unit has shown you four different ways of creating a web page. There are lots of other programs that you could also choose from. The problem you have is knowing which one is the best option. You might think about:

> how much the software costs
> how easy each method is
> how long you think it would take to make a web page using each method
> how confident you are using the different methods.

There is no right or wrong answer about which method to choose. You should choose the method that you think is most suitable.

 End of Unit Activity: Creating a web page

In this activity you will be asked to create a web page using whichever method you choose. Open the 'Creating a web page' worksheet on the website and follow the instructions.

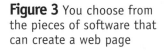 **Figure 3** You choose from the pieces of software that can create a web page

2.3 | Creating a web page using HTML

In this unit you will learn:
> **How HTML can be used to display the contents of web pages**
> **How tags are used in HTML code**
> **How you can create hyperlinks using HTML code**
> **How to create a simple web page**

Introduction

Figure 1 Using HTML code

In Unit 2.2, we looked at several ways of creating web pages. All these methods used HTML. You can either write the HTML yourself, or you can use software such as Microsoft Word, Microsoft Publisher or Microsoft FrontPage, which will create the HTML code for you. Most people choose to use software to create web pages as it is easier than learning HTML code.

It is useful to understand the basics of how HTML works and in this unit you create a basic web page by typing in HTML code.

HTML basics

We saw an example of HTML code in Unit 2.2. One of the advantages of using HTML is that you can make a web page without any specialised software. All you need is a text editor such as Notepad (which comes free with Windows) and a browser (e.g. Internet Explorer or Mozilla).

With HTML you have to type in everything as an instruction. These instructions are called HTML code. You type them into Notepad and then display the results in your browser.

HTML uses **tags**. For example, to display the text 'My first HTML web page' on a web page you would type:

```
<HTML>
<p> My first HTML web page </p>
</HTML>
```

So what does this code mean?

> `<HTML>` means that this is the start of the web page.
> `<p>` means the start of a paragraph.
> `</p>` means the end of a paragraph.
> `</HTML>` means it is the end of the web page.

There are lots of tags that you can use to add different things to the web page. For example:

> `<Head></Head>` is used to add a heading. You would type the text for the heading between the two tags, e.g. `<Head>Welcome to my web page</Head>`.
> `<Body></Body>` is used for the main displayed section of the page. You type the content that you want visitors to see between the tags.
> `<img src=>` is used to display an image. You put the name of the file that contains the image after the = sign, e.g. `<img src="Picture of me.jpg">`.
> `<b></b>` makes text bold, e.g. `<b>Hello</b>` would be displayed as **Hello**.

 Written Task: Cracking the code

In this task you will be asked to identify some HTML code. Open the 'Cracking the code' worksheet on the website and follow the instructions.

Creating hyperlinks

The code to create a hyperlink looks like this:

```
<p>Click <a href = "http://www.bbc.co.uk">here</a> to go
to the BBC website</p>
```

> The `<p>` and `</p>` start and end the paragraph.
> The `<a>` stands for anchor and it fixes the link to this text.
> The `"href"` is where you put the name of the web page that you want to link to.
> The `</a>` means that this is the end of the hyperlink.

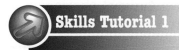 **Skills Tutorial 1** This tutorial shows you how to use Notepad to create a web page.

 End of Unit Activity: My favourite websites

In this activity you will be asked to create a web page using HTML code. Open the 'My favourite websites' worksheet on the website and follow the instructions.

2.4 | Creating a web page using specialised software

Learning Objectives

In this unit you will learn how to:
> **Create a web page using specialised software**
> **Build a website**
> **Apply a consistent design theme**
> **Add pages and links**

Introduction

Specialised software such as Microsoft FrontPage or Adobe Dreamweaver can be used for creating web pages. The advantage of using specialised software is that they have more web design features in them than Microsoft Word or Microsoft Publisher.

In this unit, we will look at some of these specific features. This unit will use Microsoft FrontPage as an example. Other web design software is available and you may have access to it in your school. You will find that all web design software will have the same basic features, but that some might have more advanced options. Adobe Dreamweaver for example has many more options than FrontPage and so is more expensive to buy.

Standard features

Many of the standard features of web design software are the same as other software you are used to. For example, you create a design on a blank page, adding text and graphics and re-sizing and positioning everything how you want it.

You may already have used Microsoft FrontPage in Unit 2.2.

 **Skills Tutorial 1** This tutorial shows you how to use Microsoft FrontPage to create a web page.

 Written Task: Designing a personal web page
In this task you will be asked to plan the design for a personal web page. Open the 'Designing a personal web page' worksheet on the website and follow the instructions.

Practical Task: Creating a personal web page

In this task you will be asked to create a personal web page. Open the 'Creating a personal web page' worksheet on the website and follow the instructions.

Using themes and styles

If you are going to create several pages, you should think about the overall style that you plan to use. For example, when you make a PowerPoint presentation, you usually have the same background colour on every slide and you use the same font styles and sizes on each slide. Your web pages should also have a consistent theme.

You can do this yourself by making sure you are consistent, or you can set a **theme**. Using a theme means that the style of every web page will be the same. For example, if you add a heading to each page, it ensures that the heading uses exactly the same font style, colour and size for every page. If you add a background, it ensures that it is exactly the same colour and pattern.

Figure 1 Using styles

 **Skills Tutorial 2** | This tutorial shows you how to apply a theme to a web page and use styles.

Adding and linking pages

Most websites consist of several web pages. As new pages are added, the links need to be created to and from this new page. You can add hyperlinks to any text or image. You can also set up a **button** to act as a hyperlink.

For example, the web page below has a number of buttons (the yellow rectangles) that link to different pages. One of the advantages of using the buttons is that you can have the same set of buttons on every page, which makes it easy for people to navigate around your site.

Figure 2 Button links

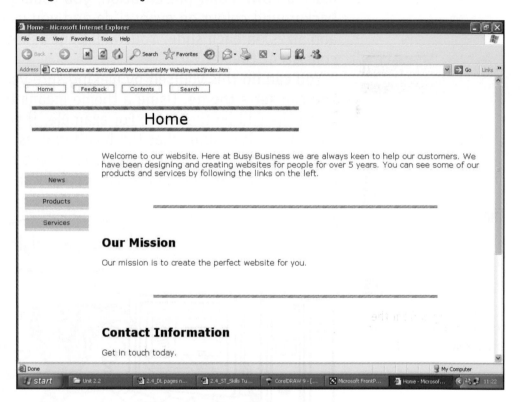

This website was created using the wizard in FrontPage. Wizards are useful because they do a lot of the work for you. The problem with them is that they might not produce exactly want you want. This design, for example, has a lot of white space and no images.

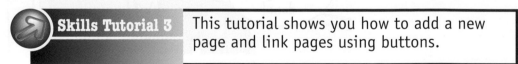

Skills Tutorial 3 This tutorial shows you how to add a new page and link pages using buttons.

You should ensure that you apply the same theme and use the same styles on the new page and on every other page you create for this website. As you create new pages, you need to add new hyperlinks between the new page and existing pages.

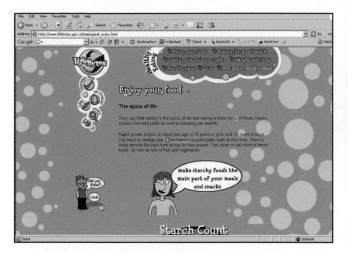
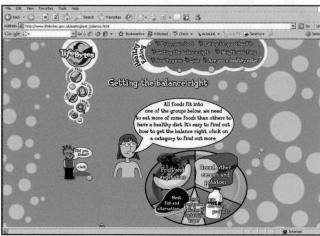
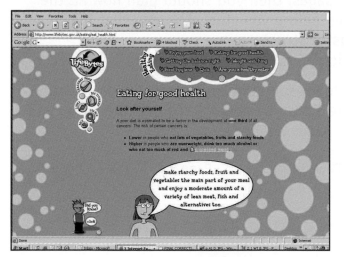
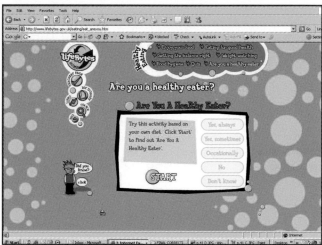

Figure 3 Pages from the Healthy Eating section of the LifeBytes website

End of Unit Activity: Developing a website

In this activity you will be asked to create a website made up of several web pages. Open the 'Developing a website' worksheet on the website and follow the instructions.

2.5 | Structuring a website

In this unit you will learn how to:
> **Design websites with a clear structure**
> **Make your website easy to navigate**

Introduction

In the previous units we have created a web page and then linked new web pages to build a website. If you know that you are going to be creating several pages, then you should plan how all the pages will link together before you start. The way that the pages link is called the **website structure**.

There are three basic structures:

> **Linear** – one page follows another in sequence (see Figure 1, where hyperlinks are shown by arrows). To get to page 4, you have to go through pages 2 and 3.

Figure 1 Linear website structure

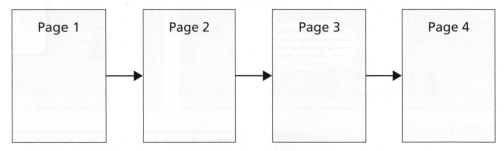

Figure 2 Tree structure

> **Tree** – the structure is like a family tree (see Figure 3). Page 1 is a main page with links to the other three pages. There is no direct link between page 2 and page 3, for example.

Figure 3 Tree website structure

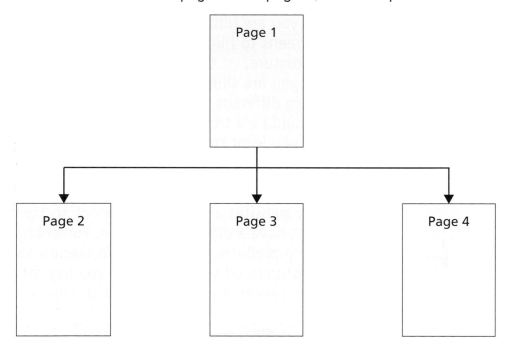

> **Random** – any page can link directly to any other page. In Figure 4, every page contains a hyperlink to every other page.

Figure 4 Random website structure

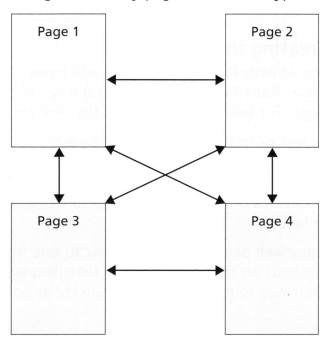

Choosing the appropriate structure

Web designers choose the most suitable structure depending on what the website is for. For example:

> If you are filling in an online form, you might be shown several screens to fill in, one after another. This would be a linear structure.
> If you are shopping online, the products might be organised into different categories to make them easier to find. This would be a tree structure.
> If you want to look for information using an online encyclopedia, each page will contain links to other related topics. This would be a random structure.

Many websites are built in different sections and each section might have a different structure. For example, when you are buying products online, the information about the products is in tree-structured sections. When you pay for the products, the linear checkout is in a different section of the website.

Written Task: Website structures

In this task you will be asked to look at how websites are structured. Open the 'Website structures' worksheet on the website and follow the instructions.

Creating the links

You already know that you can add hyperlinks anywhere on a page. Many websites have several ways of linking to the same page. For example you can put the link on:

> text or images within a web page
> buttons that are usually arranged down the left or across the top of every page
> buttons that appear at the bottom of a page, e.g. a Next button
> tabs.

Many web pages, such as the Tiscali one in Figure 5, use all these methods on the same page, so that people using the site can find their way round as easily and quickly as possible.

Figure 5 Website with multiple types of structure

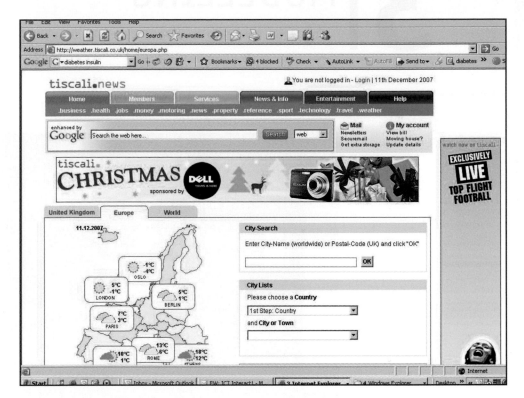

It has tabs across the top of the page (e.g. Home, members and so on), links on almost every piece of text (usually shown in blue) and it also has a search box, in case you can't find what you want on the page. Other pages, such as picture galleries, will have 'Previous' and 'Next' buttons to scroll through the pictures.

 End of Unit Activity: Structuring a website

In this activity you will be asked to create a structure for a website. Open the 'Structuring a website' worksheet on the website and follow the instructions.

 End of Module Assignment: Creating a website

In this assignment you will be asked to design and create a website from scratch. You should then ask someone to review your website and make any further changes. Open the 'Module 2 assignment' worksheet on the website and follow the instructions.

3 MODELLING

Figure 1 Harriet outside her diner

This is Harriet. She is the proud owner of the Yellow Belly Diner, a popular 100-seater restaurant. The restaurant is styled on an American Diner. It is open every day from 10 a.m. to 10 p.m. Harriet employs quite a few staff. Many of these are part-time and work shifts. This is useful to Harriet as sometimes the restaurant is busier than at other times.

> **Q** Why might Harriet need more staff when the diner is busy? When do you think the busiest times and days are likely to be?

Harriet has found that Sundays are very busy as people like to eat out at the weekend. In fact, Sunday lunchtime is usually the busiest time of the week with people queuing for seats. Harriet has extra workers in on a Sunday to serve on tables. She sometimes has 12 or 13 waiters or waitresses working on a Sunday lunchtime. By contrast, Monday morning is almost dead. Sometimes the staff are sitting around with nothing to do because it is so quiet. She probably only needs two or three waiters or waitresses to work on a Monday.

> **Q** If you were Harriet, how would you work out how many staff to have working on different days of the week?

Harriet has worked out that she needs an average of six members of staff working each day. However, sometimes six is too many and sometimes it is not enough.

She looks at the number of customers that she gets in the typical week. She has typed this into a spreadsheet.

Figure 2 Customers per day in the diner

	A	B	C	D	E
1	**Number of customers this month**				
2					
3		Week 1	Week 2	Week 3	Week 4
4	Monday	203	234	287	254
5	Tuesday	290	270	264	243
6	Wednesday	256	297	276	256
7	Thursday	345	387	378	389
8	Friday	325	389	364	327
9	Saturday	657	634	689	647
10	Sunday	857	980	894	978
11					

> **Q** Can you see any pattern in the data? Which days seem to be the busiest? How can this help Harriet work out how many staff to have on each day?

Harriet already knows that one waiter or waitress can serve about 80 people per day. So if she gets 240 customers in a day, she would need three staff. The problem is that she can't be sure exactly how many customers she might get in a typical day. However, she can make a prediction based on the numbers she already has.

> **Q** How else could Harriet present these data to make them easier to read?

Harriet decides to graph the data to make it easier to see the pattern. She produces a grouped bar chart.

Figure 3 Graph of customers per day in the diner

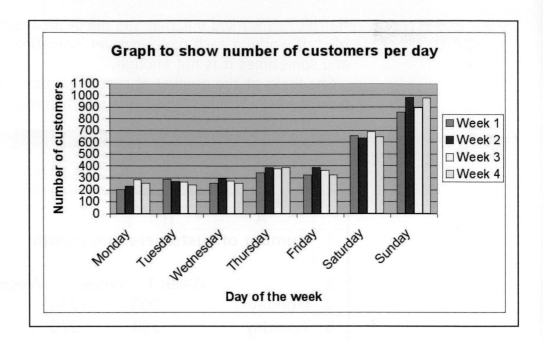

> **Q** Which are the quietest days of the week? How many customers do they get on a typical Tuesday? How many customers do they get on a typical Saturday?

Harriet decides to create a spreadsheet model to predict how many customers there will be in the restaurant each day. She could then use this to work out how many staff to have on duty each day. She does not know exactly how many customers she will get each day, but she can get the computer to predict the number. For example, on Monday she knows it could be anywhere between 200 and 300. She sets up the model to generate a random number between 200 and 300. She then divides this by 80 to work out how many staff to have on duty.

In this example, the model predicts there will be 287 customers and that she needs four staff on duty. Harriet runs the model over and over again to simulate what might happen in real life. She runs the model a few more times.

Microsoft Excel - Module 3_MA_Yellow Belly Diner Model.xls

File   Edit   View   Insert   Format   Tools   Data   Window   Help

Reply with Changes... End Review...

G14

	A	B	C
1	**Yellow Belly Diner**		
2			
3		Predicted number of customers	Number of staff needed
4	Monday	287	4

Figure 4 Predicted customers

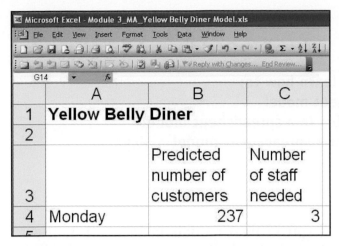

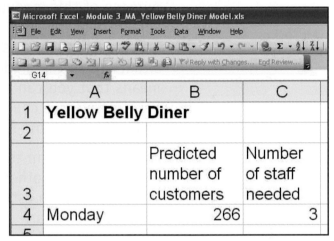

Figure 5 More customer predictions

Q How many members of staff do you think Harriet needs for a typical Monday?

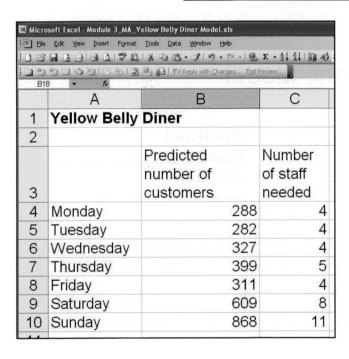

	Predicted number of customers	Number of staff needed
Yellow Belly Diner		
Monday	288	4
Tuesday	282	4
Wednesday	327	4
Thursday	399	5
Friday	311	4
Saturday	609	8
Sunday	868	11

Figure 6 shows the finished model.

Harriet is very pleased with the model and she uses it to decide how many members of staff she should have on each day. She finds that it works well.

Q How realistic do you think a model like this is? How could the model be extended to be even more useful to Harriet? What other situations could be modelled in this way?

Figure 6 Finished model

49

3.1 Creating a spreadsheet model

In this unit you will learn how to:
> **Create a spreadsheet model**
> **Set up the variables in a spreadsheet model**
> **Set up the rules in a spreadsheet model**

Introduction

We covered the basics of spreadsheet models in InteraCT 1. The purpose of this module is to design and create more complex spreadsheet models.

Spreadsheet models are useful because you can recreate real-life situations in the model and then ask **what if** questions. This means that you can make predictions about what might happen. For example, we could build a model (Figure 1) to predict how much it might cost for a mobile phone.

> We could put in the price of the phone, the cost of texts and calls and any other charges.
> We could then estimate how many calls and texts we expect to make each year.
> The model will then work out the total costs over the year.
> We can change the model to try out different phones and tariffs.

Figure 1 Mobile phone model

Microsoft Excel - 3.1_A_Mobile Phone Model.xls

File Edit View Insert Format Tools Data Window Help

	A	B	C	D	E
1	**Mobile Phone Model**				
2					
3	**Charges**	**Amount**	**Predicted number over one year**	**Totals**	
4	Price of phone	£ 89.99	-	£ 89.99	
5	Cost of texts	£ 0.10	1800	£ 180.00	
6	Cost of calls	£ 0.25	1000	£ 250.00	
7					
8	Total cost			£ 519.99	
9					

Figure 2 Different phone costs

	Microsoft Excel - 3.1_A_Mobile Phone Model.xls			
	File Edit View Insert Format Tools Data Window Help			
	F12	fx		

	A	B	C	D	E
1	**Mobile Phone Model**				
2					
3	**Charges**	**Amount**	**Predicted number over one year**	**Totals**	
4	Price of phone	£ 129.99	-	£ 129.99	
5	Cost of texts	£ 0.10	1800	£ 180.00	
6	Cost of calls	£ 0.20	1000	£ 200.00	
7					
8	Total cost			£ 509.99	

This model would be really useful to help you decide which is the best mobile phone deal for you to choose.

In the example in Figure 1, the price of the phone is cheaper than in the example in Figure 2. You might think that this would be the cheapest option. However, once you add in the cost of the texts and calls, you can see that the second option would probably be cheaper overall.

Figure 3 Using mobile phones

Figure 4 The iPhone – changing the way mobile phones are used

Identifying the variables

The first stage of setting up a model is to decide on what **variables** you need to make the model work. A variable is a value that you might want to change when using the model. In the example above there are five variables:

> the cost of the phone
> the cost of texts
> the cost of calls
> the predicted number of texts per year
> the predicted number of calls per year.

Once you have decided on the variables, you can then start to design the spreadsheet.

 Written Task: Identifying variables

In this task you will be asked to identify what variables are needed for a spreadsheet model. Open the 'Identifying variables' worksheet on the website and follow the instructions.

Setting up the rules

The rules of a model state how the formulae are used to find the answers that we need. The rules of the mobile phone model are:

> Cost of texts x Number of texts = Total cost of texts

For example, if texts cost 10p each and you expect to send about 1800 a year this will cost you £180.

> Cost of calls x Number of calls = Total cost of calls

For example, if calls cost 20p each and you expect to make about 1000 calls a year this will cost you £200.

> Total cost of texts + Total cost of calls + Cost of phone = Total Cost

For example, you have £180 worth of texts, plus £200 of calls plus £129.99 for the cost of the phone. Add it all together and you find out the total cost of owning that phone, which is £509.99 in this example.

If we look at the formulae used in the model (Figure 5), you can see how this has been set up.

Figure 5 Formulae in mobile phone model

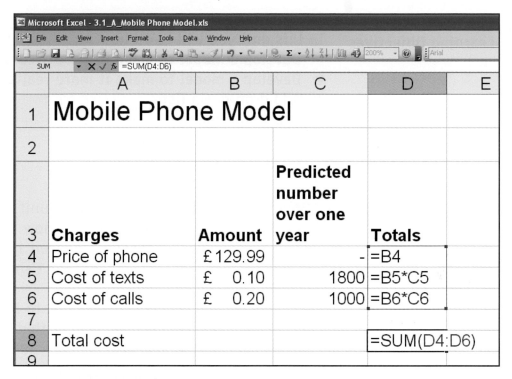

	A	B	C	D	E
1	**Mobile Phone Model**				
2					
3	**Charges**	**Amount**	**Predicted number over one year**	**Totals**	
4	Price of phone	£ 129.99	-	=B4	
5	Cost of texts	£ 0.10	1800	=B5*C5	
6	Cost of calls	£ 0.20	1000	=B6*C6	
7					
8	Total cost			=SUM(D4:D6)	
9					

Figure 6 Which mobile phone is cheaper?

The phone was free but the calls cost a fortune!

 End of Unit Activity: Setting up a model

In this activity you will be asked to set up a spreadsheet model. Open the 'Setting up a model' worksheet on the website and follow the instructions.

3.2 | Developing a model to improve accuracy

Learning Objectives

In this unit you will learn how to:
> Develop a model to make it more accurate
> Develop a model to make it more realistic
> Add drop-down lists
> Use If statements

Introduction

Microsoft Excel - 3.1_A_Concert Hall Evacuation Model (suggested solution).xls

File   Edit   View   Insert   Format   Tools   Data   Window   Help

	A	B	C
1	**Concert Hall Evacuation Model**		
2			
3	Number in hall	3000	
4	Number of fire exits	3	
5	Number evacuated per minute	100	
6	Total evacuated per minute	300	
7			
8	Total evacuation time (mins)	10	
9			
10			
11			

Figure 1 Concert hall model

In the previous unit, you created a model that estimated how long it would take to evacuate a concert hall after a fire alarm goes off. Figure 1 shows one possible solution.

For this model to be useful to us, we need to be sure that it is accurate and realistic:

> **Accurate:** Does the model give an accurate and reliable result? For example, it assumes that 100 people can be evacuated out of each exit in one minute. Do we know that this is accurate? How could we test it?

> **Realistic:** Do we think that the model recreates what might happen in real life? Is there anything else we should take into account?

Developing a model

To make models as useful as possible they have to recreate real-life situations as closely as they can. This model could be used to decide how many fire exits there should be on new buildings, which could save lives. However, if the model is wrong then it could be serious.

It is important that the model includes all possibilities. For example, a concert hall might have chairs set out for a more formal concert, but for a pop concert, there might only be standing space. If there are chairs set out, then it will probably take longer to get everyone out of the building. We can build this into the model (see Figure 2).

Skills Tutorial 1

This tutorial shows you how to add a drop-down list to a cell in Microsoft Excel.

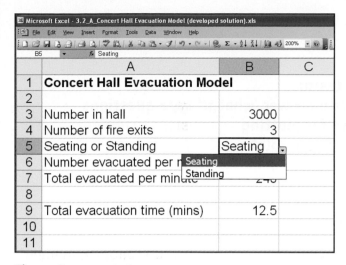

Figure 2 Concert hall model: layout options

A new row (Row 5) has been added. It contains a drop-down list to show whether the event uses 'Seating' or whether it is 'Standing' only.

The drop-down list is a useful feature because the person using the model can only choose one of the options listed – they cannot type anything else into this cell. This means that the only two choices in this case are 'Seating' and 'Standing'.

The formula in cell B6 has been changed:

> If it is a 'Seating' concert then the 'Number evacuated per minute' is 80. This is because it will take people longer to get to the exits.
> If it is a 'Standing' concert, then the 'Number evacuated per minute' is 100.

Figure 3 Concert hall model: seating layout

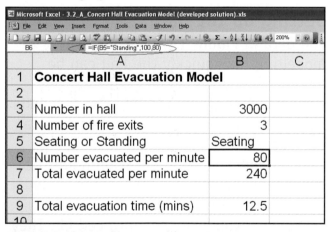

If statements

The formula used to set the value in cell B6 is called an **If statement**:

=IF (B5='Standing',100,80)

This means that if the value in cell B5 is 'Standing' then the value in cell B6 is 100. If the value in cell B5 is anything else (and it can only be 'Seating' in this case), then the value of B6 is set to 80.

Skills Tutorial 2

This tutorial shows you how to create an If statement in Microsoft Excel.

Written Task: Checking a model

In this task you will be asked to check how accurate and realistic a spreadsheet model is. Open the 'Checking a model' worksheet on the website and follow the instructions.

End of Unit Activity: Developing the mobile phone model

In this activity you will be asked to improve a spreadsheet model. Open the 'Developing the mobile phone model' worksheet on the website and follow the instructions.

3.3 | Using graphs to model data

Learning Objectives

In this unit you will learn:
> **How graphs can help answer 'what if' type questions**
> **How to set up data for plotting**
> **How to select the data to plot**

Introduction

Models are used to answer 'what if' type questions. The concert hall evacuation model was useful because it could be used to work out how many fire exits there should be. We were able to use the model to answer questions such as:

> What if there were five exits?
> What if it was a seating-only concert?

We found out the answer to these questions by looking at the information in the spreadsheet model.

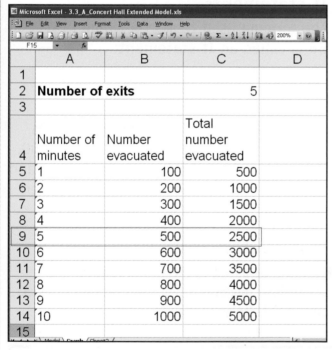

Figure 1 Concert hall model with a variable number of exits

Setting up the data

The data in Figure 1 show another way of modelling how quickly the hall can be emptied if the fire alarm goes off. They show us what effect adding extra fire exits has on the speed that the concert hall can be evacuated.

An example 'what if' question might be: 'What if we have five exits? How quickly can we evacuate the hall?'

The user would type '5' into cell C2. They could then look down the table to find out how long it would take to empty the hall depending on how full it was.

Figure 1 shows that, if the hall had 2500 people in it, they could empty it in five minutes.

Written Task: Setting up data

In this task you will be asked to set up some data in a spreadsheet model. Open the 'Setting up data' worksheet on the website and follow the instructions.

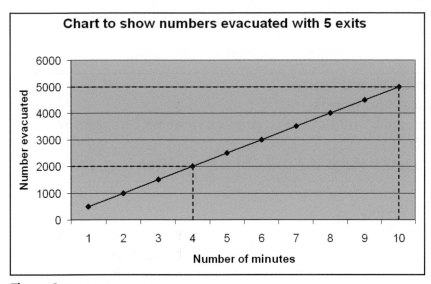

Figure 2 Graph of concert hall data with five exits

Graphing the data

It can be easier to read data from a graph instead of looking at the numbers themselves. For example, the line graph in Figure 2 has been created from the data in Figure 1.

You can now ask the same kind of 'what if' questions. The red dotted lines have been added to show you two examples:

> If the hall has 5000 people in it, it will take 10 minutes to empty it.
> If the hall has 2000 people in it, it will take four minutes to empty it.

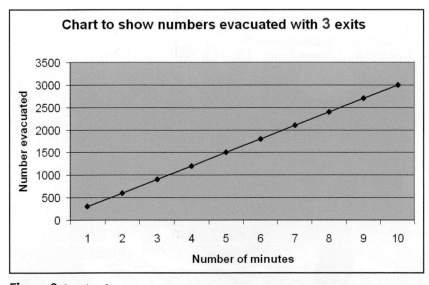

Figure 3 Graph of concert hall data with three exits

The advantage of using a graph is that you can read data directly from it and as the data change, so does the graph. Figure 3 shows the same model, but this time it looks at what will happen if there are only three exits. In this case, it would take 10 minutes to evacuate the hall if there were 3000 people in it.

 **Skills Tutorial 1** | This tutorial shows you how to set up the concert hall graph in Microsoft Excel.

 End of Unit Activity: Graphing data
In this activity you will be asked to graph data in a spreadsheet model. Open the 'Graphing data' worksheet on the website and follow the instructions.

3.4 | Using simulations

Learning Objectives

In this unit you will learn:
> What a simulation is
> How to use a simulation to predict what will happen in real life
> How to understand the rules of a simulation

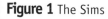

Introduction

So far in this module, we have created computer models that re-create real-life situations on the computer. Once you have set up a model you can use it to predict what will happen in real life. This is known as a **simulation**.

For example, many computer games are simulations. One well-known game is The Sims (Figure 1). In this game you create characters, and based on the choices you make about them, they behave in different ways. For example you may fall out with other characters, or if you get on really well, you might even get married.

Figure 1 The Sims

Variables and Rules

Simulations are the results of using a model. As you know, models are built using variables and rules. In a game such as The Sims there will be hundreds of variables and rules.

Another example of a computer simulation is a flight simulator (Figure 2). Examples of variables in a flight simulator are:

> weather conditions
> visibility
> speed.

Examples of rules in a flight simulator might be:

> as the accelerator stick is pushed, the plane goes faster
> pulling the main stick back makes the plane go higher.

If you can understand the variables and rules in a model, it makes it easier to 'win' the game.

Figure 2 Flight simulator

 Written Task: Variables and rules

In this task you will be asked to work out what variables and rules are needed in a spreadsheet model. Open the 'Variables and rules' worksheet on the website and follow the instructions.

Skills Tutorial 1

This tutorial shows you how to use the Investment Manager simulation.

Simulations in Excel

It is possible to create simulations of real life using Excel. You do not get all the graphics that you would get in a computer game, but you have variables and rules. We are going to use a simulation called 'Investment Manager'. The idea of the simulation is to decide how to invest your money to get as much money back as possible.

You can invest up to £10,000. The simulation gives you four investment options. Some are more risky than others. For example:

> You could play safe and put all your money in a savings account. The most likely result would be that you would make a small amount of money.
> You could take a higher risk and gamble it. You could make much more money this way, or you could lose the lot.
> You could spread your money across all four options to see what might happen.

Once you have made your choices, you can see what the predicted result would be from your investments.

For example, Figure 3 shows a fairly safe investment with £5000 in a savings account and £5000 in premium bonds. The predicted result of this is shown at the bottom. Over five years, this person would make £1027.87 on their investment.

Figure 3 Investment Manager: safe investments and predicted results

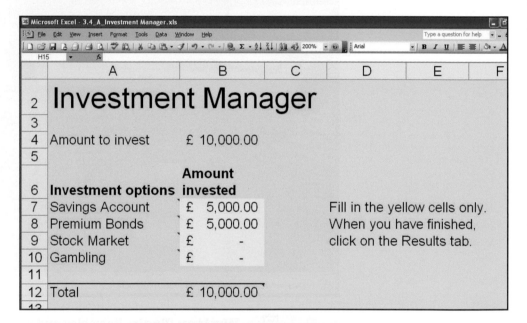

Investment Manager

	A	B
4	Amount to invest	£ 10,000.00
6	**Investment options**	**Amount invested**
7	Savings Account	£ 5,000.00
8	Premium Bonds	£ 5,000.00
9	Stock Market	£ -
10	Gambling	£ -
12	Total	£ 10,000.00

Fill in the yellow cells only. When you have finished, click on the Results tab.

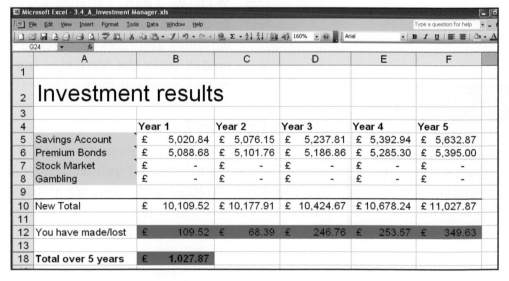

Investment results

	A	Year 1	Year 2	Year 3	Year 4	Year 5
5	Savings Account	£ 5,020.84	£ 5,076.15	£ 5,237.81	£ 5,392.94	£ 5,632.87
6	Premium Bonds	£ 5,088.68	£ 5,101.76	£ 5,186.86	£ 5,285.30	£ 5,395.00
7	Stock Market	£ -	£ -	£ -	£ -	£ -
8	Gambling	£ -	£ -	£ -	£ -	£ -
10	New Total	£ 10,109.52	£ 10,177.91	£ 10,424.67	£ 10,678.24	£ 11,027.87
12	You have made/lost	£ 109.52	£ 68.39	£ 246.76	£ 253.57	£ 349.63
18	Total over 5 years	£ 1,027.87				

Figure 4 shows the investments of someone who has chosen to gamble all their money. The simulation predicts that they could gain £515.46 in Year 1. However, because gambling is risky, if they carried on over five years, it is predicted that they would lose nearly all their money (£9645.95).

Figure 4 Investment Manager: risky investments and predicted results

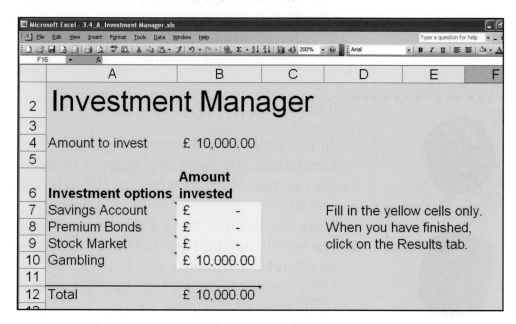

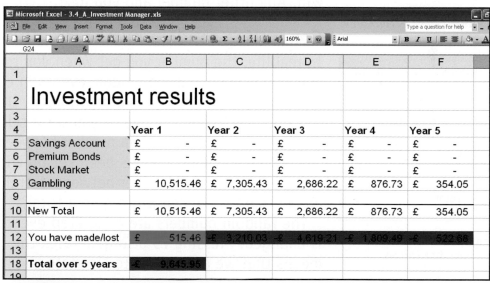

 End of Unit Activity: Understanding Investment Manager

In this task you will be asked to work out how the Investment Manager spreadsheet model works. Open the 'Understanding Investment Manager' worksheet on the website and follow the instructions.

3.5 Creating a simulation

In this unit you will learn:
> How to create a simulation
> How to use random numbers
> How to use conditional formatting
> More on If statements

Introduction

In this unit, we will work through the process of creating a simulation. The first thing to do is to build a spreadsheet model. We can then use this model to simulate what might happen in real life.

We are going to make a dice-throwing game using two dice. A die has six numbers on it. You have an equal chance of throwing any number between 1 and 6. If you are throwing two dice, the combined total can be anywhere between 2 and 12.

The rules of the game are simple – if you throw a 7 or an 11 you win. Any other number and you lose.

Figure 1 Dice game: throw 7 or 11 to win

Generating random numbers

In real life, the number you get when you roll dice is random. A common way of creating random events in computer models is to use a random number generator. In Excel, there is a function called RANDBETWEEN. For example, if you set a cell to RANDBETWEEN (1,6), it generates a random number between 1 and 6.

The model in Figure 2 has been set up with two dice. Each one generates a random number between 1 and 6. The numbers are added together in cell B6 to give a total.

The random numbers are generated every time the spreadsheet is changed. Pressing F9 also generates the numbers again. This means that we can use F9 to simulate the rolling of the dice.

	A	B
1	**The Dice Game**	
2		
3	Die 1	4
4	Die 2	6
5		
6	Total	10
7		

Figure 2 Generator of random dice throws

Skills Tutorial 1

This tutorial shows you how to use the RANDBETWEEN function.

Written Task: Random numbers
In this task you will be asked questions about the use of random numbers in a spreadsheet. Open the 'Random numbers' worksheet on the website and follow the instructions.

Conditional Formatting

We can add formatting to the model. If we throw a 7 or 11, we win. We can set up the formatting to show when we have won. One way of doing this is to make cell B6 go a different colour if we throw a winning number.

Excel has a feature called **conditional formatting**. It sets the formatting of the cell if the value is a certain amount. In this example, it sets the cell colour to bright green if the value in the cell is 7 (Figure 3).

Figure 3 Conditional formatting

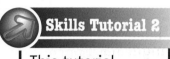

Skills Tutorial 2

This tutorial shows you how to add conditional formatting to a cell.

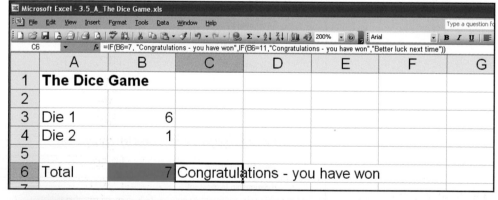

If statements

Another way of showing when we have won is to use an If statement to put a comment in one of the cells. Look at cell C6 in Figure 4. If the value in cell B6 is a 7 or an 11, it reads 'Congratulations – you have won'. If not, it reads 'Better luck next time'.

Figure 4 Using an If statement to show a comment

Skills Tutorial 3

This tutorial shows you how to create an If statement.

	A	B	C	D	E	F	G
1	**The Dice Game**						
2							
3	Die 1	6					
4	Die 2	1					
5							
6	Total	7	Congratulations - you have won				

C6 fx =IF(B6=7, "Congratulations - you have won",IF(B6=11,"Congratulations - you have won","Better luck next time"))

 End of Unit Activity: Card game simulation

In this activity you will be asked to use a spreadsheet simulation. Open the 'Card game simulation' worksheet on the website and follow the instructions.

 End of Module Assignment: Airline model

In this assignment you will be asked to create a spreadsheet model for an airline. You will then use the model to create graphs. Open the 'Module 3 assignment' worksheet on the website and follow the instructions.

Case Study introduction

AgeProof provide ID cards for young people aged 15 and 16. They are photo ID cards that prove that the person with the card is 15 or older. The ID cards are popular with 15- and 16-year-olds who often have to prove their age. For example, it means that they can get into a 15-certificate film or that they don't have to pay an adult fare on a train or bus.

> **Q** What information do you think AgeProof are going to need before they can issue an ID card? Where will they get this information?

Figure 1 Application form

Application form for an AgeProof ID card

Part A Applicant to complete this section

First name

Last name

Gender   Male   Female

Home Address

Postcode

Email address

Telephone Number

Date of Birth

Today's Date

For urgent application, tick here.

Part B Parent/Guardian to complete this section

Parent's Full Name

Relationship to applicant

Today's Date

This is the form that AgeProof normally use. When a young person applies for an ID card, AgeProof email them this form as an attachment. The young person then prints it off, fills it in and sends it back. Someone at AgeProof then types the young person's details into the AgeProof computer.

> **Q** What problems might there be with this way of getting the forms filled in? How could they solve these problems?

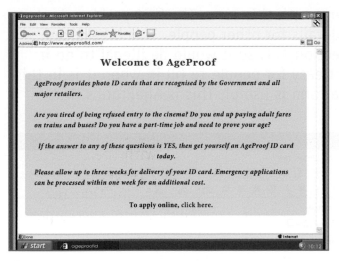

Figure 2 AgeProof home page

AgeProof have decided to let young people apply for their ID cards on their website. They have set up a link on their home page. Doing it online means that young people will not have to print and send any paperwork. The young person can fill in the form online and the information can be stored straight into a database. AgeProof realise that it is important to set this all up carefully as lots of people will be using the website and there will be lots of data to collect and store. There are two things they need to do: set up the database and set up the form.

> **Q** What fields do they need to store? What data types should they use for each field? What validation checks should there be on each field?

Figure 3 Design view of AgeProof database

AgeProof are using database software to collect the data. The software they are using is called Microsoft Access. This screen shows how they have set up the data. In Access, this is known as a **table**. Each field is listed and the data type is also shown. This view is called the Design view because it is where the database is designed. The view shown in Figure 4 is called the Datasheet view and it is where people fill in their details.

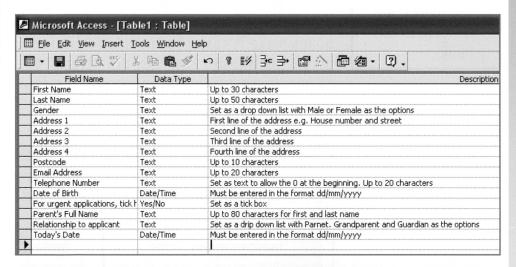

Figure 4 Datasheet view of AgeProof database

Q What problems might there be in asking people to fill in their data on this screen?

Figure 5 First attempt at the data collection form

There are a few problems with this view. The first problem is that you can see personal details for other people. This breaks the rules of the Data Protection Act, so it would be illegal to do it like this. Also, it is not easy for people to fill in when it is in this format. This is where a form is useful. This is AgeProof's first attempt at a form:

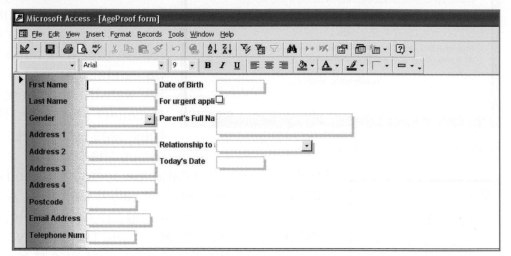

Q What improvements do you think could be made to this form?

Figure 6 shows the final version of the form that AgeProof will be putting on their website. It will link directly to the database that they have set up. It is now laid out and formatted much more professionally and features such as the drop-down lists and tick boxes make it easier for people to fill in. AgeProof put the form up on the website and they are pleased to find out that hundreds of people are using it. Very soon their database has over 10,000 people in it and they are able to use the information to send out ID cards to all the people who apply.

Figure 6 Final version of the data collection form

Q How else could AgeProof use the information stored in the database?

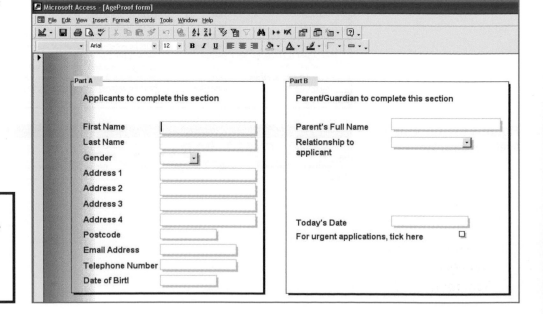

Figure 7 shows a small sample of the 10,000 records that AgeProof have on their database. The managers at AgeProof plan to use these data to find out other things. For example: do more males than females apply for ID cards? What is the average age of people who apply for an ID card? How many of the applications are urgent?

Figure 7 Records in the AgeProof database

First Name	Last Name	Gender	Address 1	Address 2	Address 3	Postcode	Email Address	Telephone Nu	Date of Birth
Geoff	Randall	Male	1 High Street	Ransdown	Ranshire	RN1 1AA	Randall@email.com	01555 553553	07/11/199
Mary	Highe	Female	12a Long Row	Ransdown	Ranshire	RN1 4AB	Mhighe@email.com	01555 534263	08/10/199
Marie	Okanawe	Female	32 Hallow Street	Ransdown	Ranshire	RN1 3HS	MOk@email.com	01555 756473	12/12/199
Jennie	Lui	Female	12 Nelson Street	Ransdown	Ranshire	RN2 6GD	jlui@email.com	01555 655746	01/04/199
Mike	Oldham	Male	65 Terry Road	Ransdown	Ranshire	RN5 8HH	oldham@email.com	01555 233425	17/10/199
Reg	Marrakesh	Male	78 York Road	Ransdown	Ranshire	RN3 7HS	BigReg@email.com	01555 434434	21/10/199
Asif	Assan	Male	12 Jarrow Road	Ransdown	Ranshire	RN13 8GH	asif@email.com	01555 657456	13/10/199
Nancy	Cartright	Female	65 Elvin Road	Ransdown	Ranshire	RN32 7HS	nancyc@email.com	01555 123432	12/03/199
Emily	Brownhurst	Female	12 High Street	Ransdown	Ranshire	RN12 8US	emilyb@email.com	01555 098765	31/10/199
John	Connor	Male	76 Fallow Road	Ransdown	Ranshire	RN2 5TH	jc@email.com	01555 748375	07/11/199
Matt	Dullard	Male	9 The Ridings	Ransdown	Ranshire	RN8 8DD	dullard@email.com	01555 342534	03/03/199
Tolu	Owewa	Female	12 Westlake Avenue	Ransdown	Ranshire	RN12 5FD	tolu@email.com	01555 768564	12/09/199
Anila	Sarron	Female	65a Judd Street	Ransdown	Ranshire	RN7 8UU	sarron@email.com	01555 756475	01/04/199
Nigel	Brown	Male	5 Venison Way	Ransdown	Ranshire	RN5 4HH	nigebi@email.com	01555 367456	26/07/199
Linda	Lorne	Female	1 Queen Street	Ransdown	Ranshire	RN3 6FF	doubleL@email.com	01555 986574	13/10/199

> **Q** How could AgeProof use the database to find out this information? How could they present this information?

AgeProof can use the database software to search and sort through the records and to create reports and graphs of the results. The report in Figure 8 has been created for the managers of AgeProof. It shows the percentage of males and females who apply. Some of the information is shown as a graph, some as a table and there is some text to explain it as well. This report has been created in Word with the information copied and pasted across from the database software.

Figure 8 Report from the AgeProof database

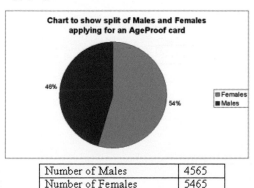

Report into the AgeProof Database

This report has been prepared for the managers of AgeProof.

This graph shows the number of people applying for AgeProof cards broken down by gender. The actual numbers are shown in the table. As you can see there are more females than males applying for ID cards.

Chart to show split of Males and Females applying for an AgeProof card

46% 54%

■ Females
■ Males

Number of Males	4565
Number of Females	5465

> **Q** How else could this information have been presented to the managers at AgeProof?

4.1 Setting up a database

In this unit you will learn how to:
> **Create a database from scratch**
> **Structure the database**
> **Use specialised database software**

Introduction

We covered the basics of databases in InteraCT 1. The purpose of this module is to design and create databases using specialised database software.

A database is a collection of data on a related topic, collected for a particular purpose.

For example, the Police National Computer (PNC) database is a collection of data about criminals and their crimes. The data have been collected to try to prevent crimes and to identify who might have committed a crime.

This is a good example of a large database with thousands of records. Putting all this information on a computer database gives a big advantage as looking through all these records by hand would take hours. The computer can do it in seconds.

Setting up a database

The first step in setting up a database is to decide what data must be collected. The next step is collecting the data. There are two main ways of getting the data:

> **Data collection (Questionnaire or Form):** Information is filled in either on paper or on-screen. We used questionnaires in InteraCT 1. A form is similar to a questionnaire. Figure 1 shows an example of a form.

> **Data capture:** This is where data are collected automatically as they are created. For example, every time someone uses a cash machine, data about the account number and how much money was taken out are stored in a database. Every time a product is scanned at a supermarket checkout, the data about that product are stored in a database.

Car Insurance Database

Title

First Name

Surname

Date of Birth

What is your marital status?

House number or name   Find address

Postcode

Email address

Telephone number

Are you employed? (tick for yes)

Do you drive for a living? (tick for yes)

Figure 1 Data collection form

Structuring the data

It is important to store data in the correct format. This is known as the data type and we looked at this in InteraCT 1. For example, looking at the online form above:

> 'Title' and 'Marital status' are stored as *multiple-choice* or *list*.
> 'Name' and 'Address' are stored as *text*.
> 'Date of birth' is stored as *date*.
> 'Do you drive for a living?' is stored as *Yes/No*.

You also need to think about how much space you leave for each answer. For example:

> 'Name' must be about 50 characters to allow for someone with a really long name.
> 'Address' must be about 100 characters, or you could split it out into separate lines.
> 'Age' can be three digits – no one can be over 999 years old.

Data validation

When data are typed into a database, there is a chance that errors will be made. For example, people might leave some fields blank, or type in values that are not valid. Data validation is a way of checking that data typed into a database fit certain rules.

For example:

> You could set age so that it can only be between 0 and 120.
> You can set the form so that all the fields must be filled in.
> You can provide people with lists of options to choose from rather than asking them to type in their answers.

Using database software

Database software is designed specially for storing and analysing data. There are different programs to choose from. We will be using Microsoft Access, which is used by many schools and businesses. You may have other software in your school, such as PinPoint, ViewPoint or FlexiDATA. All database software basically works in the same way. It lets you design forms and set up the data types. You can also search and sort through the data, which we will do in later units.

Written Task: Designing a data structure

In this task you will be asked to design a way of storing data. Open the 'Designing a data structure' worksheet on the website and follow the instructions.

Skills Tutorial 1

This tutorial shows you how to set up a database in Microsoft Access.

Skills Tutorial 2

This tutorial shows you how to add validation checks to a Microsoft Access database.

End of Unit Activity: Setting up a database

In this activity you will be asked to set up a database. Open the 'Setting up a database' worksheet on the website and follow the instructions.

4.2

Working with forms

In this unit you will learn:
> **How forms are used to collect and view data**
> **How to create a form using database software**

Introduction

We have now set up a structure for a database, but we need a user-friendly way of using it. Figure 1 shows what data look like when they are stored in a database. Here is an example of a record for John Anderson:

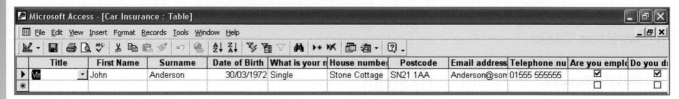

Figure 1 Data in a database

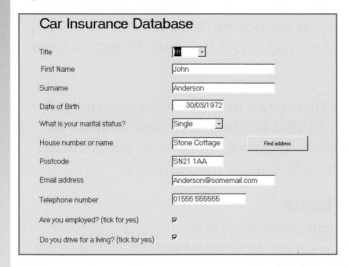

Figure 2 Data in a database form

This is where a form is useful. A form is a way of entering and viewing data in a database. Figure 2 shows John Anderson's information again, but this time it is displayed using a form.

Using forms

Forms are similar to questionnaires. They are a way of asking people for information. They can be **paper-based** or **computer-based**. Forms are used a lot online. For example, you will have to fill in a form:

> if you register your details with a website
> if you buy something online
> if you set up an email account.

All of this information will be stored on a database by whoever owns and runs the website.

Form design

In InteraCT 1 you created questionnaires. The design of the questionnaire was important. The same rules apply to the design of forms. Notice how the form shown above has been designed to make it clear and easy to fill in and read the information. For example:

> It has a clear and simple layout.
> All the information can be displayed on one screen.
> All the boxes are the correct size to display the data held in them.
> Drop-down lists mean that people fill in the form easily without making mistakes.
> Tick boxes make it quick and easy to fill in the form.
> There is information to guide people on how to fill in the form.

Skills Tutorial 1

This tutorial shows you how to create a form in Microsoft Access.

 Written Task: Designing a form

In this task you will be asked to design a form that can be used to collect data. Open the 'Designing a form' worksheet on the website and follow the instructions.

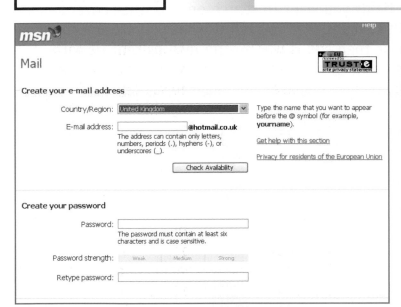

Figure 3 Typical online forms

 End of Unit Activity: Setting up a form

In this activity you will be asked to create a form that can be used to collect data. Open the 'Setting up a form' worksheet on the website and follow the instructions.

4.3 | Advanced search techniques

Querying a database

The reason for having any database is so that it can be searched to find information. For example, the police might use the PNC database to find all known burglars in a particular town.

We looked at searching in InteraCT 1 using the 'filter' option in a spreadsheet. In database software, carrying out a search is called a **query**. Therefore, querying a database means that you are searching a database.

When you carry out a query, you need to tell the database software what fields you want to search on and what criteria you want to use. This means that you tell it what you are searching for. The database then shows you all the records that fit with what you are searching for.

Figure 1 Dog Rescue charity database

Name	Colour	Breed	Size	Temperament	Age	Date rescu
Bernie	Brown	Mongrel	Medium	Loyal	2	13/06/20
Blackie	Black	Poodle	Medium	Sociable	8	15/05/20
Bod	Black and White	Shih-Tzu	Small	Loyal	5	13/06/20
Bruce	Black	Mongrel	Large	Active	7	30/05/20
Bruno	Grey	Mongrel	Medium	Loyal	2	05/12/20
Buck	Brown	Mongrel	Small	Lively	6	25/01/20
Butch	Black and White	Staffordshire Bull Terrier	Medium	Active	3	15/12/20
Cadbury	Brown	Mongrel	Medium	Sociable	4	21/05/20
Camilla	Brown and White	Mongrel	Small	Sociable	6	19/12/20
Chaucer	Brown	Red Setter	Large	Active	5	21/01/20
Chocolate Drop	Brown	Labrador	Medium	Sociable	6	25/09/20
Chuck	Brown	Mongrel	Large	Sociable	5	30/01/20
Chunk	Black	Spaniel	Small	Loyal	4	31/01/20
Cocoa	White	Mongrel	Medium	Active	3	27/10/20
Cody	Black	Labrador	Medium	Loyal	3	12/12/20
Cracker	Black and White	Dalmation	Medium	Sociable	3	04/12/20
Fido	Brown	Spaniel	Small	Loyal	1	01/11/20
Hughie	Brown and White	Mongrel	Large	Active	3	15/04/20
Jack	Brown	Staghound	Medium	Lively	7	30/01/20
Jed	Brown	Great Dane	Large	Lively	2	13/12/20
Jericho	Black	Mongrel	Small	Loyal	5	13/06/20
Kipper	Grey	Pointer	Medium	Active	4	23/05/20
Lackie	Black and White	Mongrel	Large	Active	2	26/07/20
Laddie	Black and White	Collie	Medium	Loyal	4	30/01/20
Lassie	Black and White	Mongrel	Medium	Active	5	12/12/20
Lucky	Black and White	Mongrel	Small	Active	2	20/02/20
Matty	Brown	Mongrel	Large	Sociable	6	13/06/20
Moby	Brown and White	Spaniel	Small	Loyal	3	09/01/20
Mouse	White	Labrador	Medium	Loyal	5	30/01/20
Picasso	Brown	Pointer	Pointer	Sociable	1	20/06/20
Pod	Brown and White	Saint Bernard	Large	Loyal	4	05/05/20
Reggie	Grey	Poodle	Medium	Sociable	1	20/02/20

Take a look at the database in Figure 1. It is used by a dog rescue charity.

You could use this database to carry out the following queries:

> Search for brown dogs. You would do this by entering: **Colour = "brown"**.
> Search for dogs that are aged 2 or younger. You would do this by entering: **Age <=2**.
> Search for dogs that are brown and medium sized. You would do this by entering: **Colour = "Brown" AND Size = "Medium"**.
> Search for dogs that are medium sized and loyal or sociable. You would do this by entering: **Size = "Medium" AND Temperament = "Loyal" OR "Sociable"**.

This database would be really useful for the charity to help them match dogs with new owners. For example, if someone was looking for a medium-sized, loyal dog that was less than two years old, they could quickly query the database to find all the dogs that fit the description.

Written Task: Writing queries

In this task you will be asked to write some database queries. Open the 'Writing queries' worksheet on the website and follow the instructions.

Figure 2 Write a query to find the information you want

Simple queries

A simple query usually means that you are only searching using one criterion. For example:

> **Colour = "Brown"** would list all the dogs that are brown.
> **Microchipped = "Y"** would list all the dogs that have a microchip.
> **Age BETWEEN 2 AND 5** would list all dogs that are aged 2, 3, 4 or 5 years old.

When you are doing a simple search you can use:

> The = sign, which means that you are looking for an exact match.
> The >= sign, which means that you want values greater than or equal to the value you give.
> The <= sign, which means that you want values less than or equal to the value you give.
> BETWEEN, which means the value is equal to or between the two values you give.

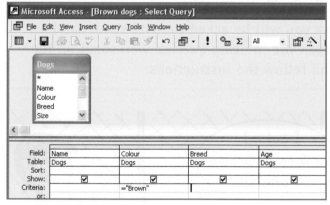

Figure 3 A simply query for brown dogs

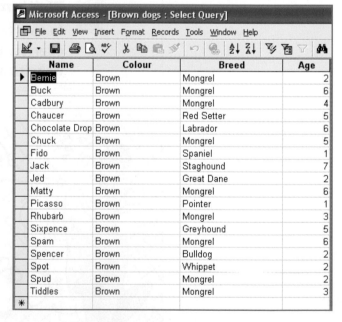

Name	Colour	Breed	Age
Bernie	Brown	Mongrel	2
Buck	Brown	Mongrel	6
Cadbury	Brown	Mongrel	4
Chaucer	Brown	Red Setter	5
Chocolate Drop	Brown	Labrador	6
Chuck	Brown	Mongrel	5
Fido	Brown	Spaniel	1
Jack	Brown	Staghound	7
Jed	Brown	Great Dane	2
Matty	Brown	Mongrel	6
Picasso	Brown	Pointer	1
Rhubarb	Brown	Mongrel	3
Sixpence	Brown	Greyhound	5
Spam	Brown	Mongrel	6
Spencer	Brown	Bulldog	2
Spot	Brown	Whippet	2
Spud	Brown	Mongrel	2
Tiddles	Brown	Mongrel	3

Skills Tutorial 1 | This tutorial shows you how to carry out queries in Microsoft Access.

Complex queries

A complex query means that you are searching using two or more criteria. You can put the criteria together using an AND or an OR. For example:

> **Colour = "Brown" OR "Brown and White"** would list all dogs that are either brown or brown and white. They could be either.
> **Colour = "Brown" AND Size = "Medium"** would list all dogs that are brown and medium sized. They have to be both.
> **Colour = "Brown" AND Size = "Medium" AND Age <=3** would list all dogs that are brown and medium-sized and aged 3 or less. They have to be all three.

As you can see, queries can get quite complicated. One good thing about database software is that you can save your queries. This means that once you have set them up, you can go back to them and edit them if you need to change the criteria.

Figure 4 A complex query for small brown dogs less than three years old

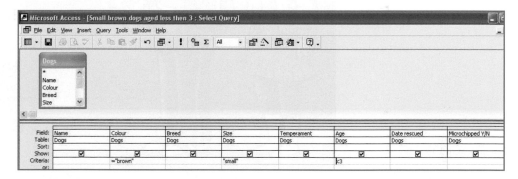

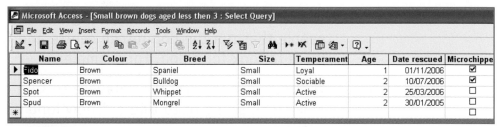

 End of Unit Activity: Querying the Dog Rescue database

In this activity you will be asked to carry out queries on a database and find the answers to some questions. Open the 'Querying the Dog Rescue database' worksheet on the website and follow the instructions.

4.4

Presenting results

In this unit you will learn how to:
> **Present results in different ways**
> **Create reports using database software**
> **Integrate data with other software**

Figure 1 I've had him microchipped!

Introduction

The Dog Rescue charity database is a really useful tool for the people that run the dog rescue centre and for the people who go there to look for a dog. For example:

> The centre can use the database to find out which dogs need microchipping or to find out how long each dog has been with them.
> People looking for a dog can put their desired characteristics into the database and it will suggest dogs they might want to look at.

It is important that the results are presented in a format that is suitable for the user. For example, at the moment the data are presented in a table. It might be useful for the information to be presented as a report.

Sometimes it might be useful to use different software to present the information stored in a database. For example, data from the database could be put into a slideshow or word-processing software.

Creating Reports

Figure 2 Dog Rescue
charity data as a table

Name	Colour	Breed	Size	Temperament
Bernie	Brown	Mongrel	Medium	Loyal
Buck	Brown	Mongrel	Small	Lively
Cadbury	Brown	Mongrel	Medium	Sociable
Chaucer	Brown	Red Setter	Large	Active
Chocolate Drop	Brown	Labrador	Medium	Sociable
Chuck	Brown	Mongrel	Large	Sociable
Fido	Brown	Spaniel	Small	Loyal
Jack	Brown	Staghound	Medium	Lively
Jed	Brown	Great Dane	Large	Lively
Matty	Brown	Mongrel	Large	Sociable
Picasso	Brown	Pointer	Pointer	Sociable
Rhubarb	Brown	Mongrel	Medium	Loyal
Sixpence	Brown	Greyhound	Medium	Lively
Spam	Brown	Mongrel	Medium	Lively
Spencer	Brown	Bulldog	Small	Sociable
Spot	Brown	Whippet	Small	Active
Spud	Brown	Mongrel	Small	Active
Tiddles	Brown	Mongrel	Medium	Sociable

At the moment the data stored in the database look like Figure 2. They are shown as a table of data. In fact they look like a spreadsheet. One advantage of using database software is that you can create a report to present the data.

A report of the same data is shown in Figure 3.

The report has some advantages over the table:

> You can add a report heading.
> There are more options for how the report is formatted and laid out.
> You can design it to fit all the information across the page (notice that Figure 2 does not show all the fields).
> It will print neatly onto A4 sheets.

You can choose to create a report of all the data in the database or you can just show certain fields. You can also create a report based on a query. For example, you could produce a report that just showed dogs that had been microchipped or that showed all dogs aged two and under.

Skills Tutorial 1	This tutorial shows you how to create a report in Microsoft Access.

Figure 3 Dog Rescue
charity data as a report

Report: All dogs at the Rescue Centre

Name	Colour	Breed	Size	Temperament	Age	Date rescued	Microchipped
Bernie	Brown	Mongrel	Medium	Loyal	2	13/06/2004	☐
Blackie	Black	Poodle	Medium	Sociable	8	15/05/2006	☑
Bod	Black and	Shih-Tzu	Small	Loyal	5	13/06/2004	☐
Bruce	Black	Mongrel	Large	Active	7	30/05/2006	☑
Bruno	Grey	Mongrel	Medium	Loyal	2	05/12/2006	☑
Buck	Brown	Mongrel	Small	Lively	6	25/01/2006	☑
Butch	Black and	Staffordshire Bull	Medium	Active	3	15/12/2006	☑
Cadbury	Brown	Mongrel	Medium	Sociable	4	21/05/2005	☐
Camilla	Brown and	Mongrel	Small	Sociable	6	19/12/2005	☐
Chaucer	Brown	Red Setter	Large	Active	5	21/01/2006	☑
Chocolate Drop	Brown	Labrador	Medium	Sociable	6	25/09/2006	☑
Chuck	Brown	Mongrel	Large	Sociable	5	30/01/2005	☐
Chunk	Black	Spaniel	Small	Loyal	4	31/01/2006	☑
Cocoa	White	Mongrel	Medium	Active	3	27/10/2006	☑
Cody	Black	Labrador	Medium	Loyal	3	12/12/2005	☐
Cracker	Black and	Dalmation	Medium	Sociable	3	04/12/2006	☑
Fido	Brown	Spaniel	Small	Loyal	1	01/11/2006	☑
Hughie	Brown and	Mongrel	Large	Active	3	15/04/2006	☑
Jack	Brown	Staghound	Medium	Lively	7	30/01/2005	☐
Jed	Brown	Great Dane	Large	Lively	2	13/12/2006	☑

Written Task: Designing a report

In this task you will be asked to design a report. Open the 'Designing a report' worksheet on the website and follow the instructions.

Figure 4 Dog Rescue
charity presentation

Older dogs

- We currently have 3 dogs aged 7 or over.

- They are difficult to find homes for as people prefer younger dogs.

- These dogs are likely to stay in the Centre.

Name	Colour	Breed	Age
Blackie	Black	Poodle	8
Bruce	Black	Mongrel	7
Jack	Brown	Staghound	7

Practical Task: Creating a report

In this task you will be asked to create a report. Open the 'Creating a report' worksheet on the website and follow the instructions.

Integrating with other software

Integrating means that you take information stored in one program and put it into another program. For example, the dog rescue centre might want to use data from the database as part of a presentation or word-processed report.

The easiest way to do this is to copy and paste. This lets you choose exactly what you want to copy from the database and then paste it directly into another program. Figure 4 shows an example from a slideshow.

In this example, the table shows the results of a query of dogs aged seven or over. The table has been copied and pasted straight from Microsoft Access. The bullet points in the presentation explain what the data mean.

Any data can be copied and pasted in this way and you can paste data into any package including Microsoft PowerPoint, Microsoft Word, Microsoft Excel, Microsoft FrontPage and Microsoft Publisher. This means, for example, that you could have data from a database presented as part of a web page.

 End of Unit Activity: Presenting results

In this activity you will be asked to analyse a database and present your results. Open the 'Presenting results' worksheet on the website and follow the instructions.

 End of Module Assignment: Swimming gala

In this assignment you will be asked to design a database that can be used to store data about a school swimming gala. Open the 'Module 4 assignment' worksheet on the website and follow the instructions.

Case Study introduction

Figure 1 Lorna standing in her drive just about to get into her car

Figure 1 Lorna standing in her drive just about to get into her car

Lorna lives on the outskirts of London. She works in London and every day she drives into the City to the office where she works. The roads in and around London are very busy and the journey is a bit of a nightmare. Lorna tries to choose the quietest roads into town and tries to avoid any traffic jams caused by accidents.

Q How could Lorna use ICT to help her with her drive into London?

Lorna has a satellite navigation (satnav) system in her car. Her mum doesn't know why she bothered buying it. Lorna has been driving into the city for the last three years, so she must know the way by now. What Lorna's mum does not realise is that the satnav also gives Lorna traffic information. This means that if one route is busy or blocked, the satnav will show her a different route.

Q How does the satellite navigation system know where Lorna is? How could the system know if there was a traffic jam?

Figure 2 Lorna with her satnav system

The satnav is telling Lorna that there is a traffic jam on the road that she normally uses, but there is another route she could take. She presses a few buttons so that the satnav tells her the new route. The new route is quite clear and the traffic is flowing freely. She is on a dual carriageway and there are lots of cars zooming down the fast lane. Lorna is always careful to stick to the speed limit.

Figure 3 Traffic flowing freely on the dual carriageway

Q How could computers be used to catch speeding drivers?

There is a speed camera on this road. If it catches someone speeding, in a few weeks time they will get a letter through the post from the police. They will get a fine and some points on their licence for speeding.

Q How does the speed camera work? How does the speed camera know whose car it is? How does the speed camera know who is driving?

Because Lorna lives and drives in London she has to pay a congestion charge. This means that if she drives into a certain area called the congestion zone, she has to pay the council. She has to pay this charge every time she enters the zone. The idea of the congestion charge is to try to discourage people from driving and to use public transport instead.

Figure 4 Congestion zone charge

Q How will the council know whether Lorna has driven into the congestion zone? How will the council know whether Lorna has paid or not?

Lorna still uses her car to get to work because the company she works for has a secure car park where she can park for free. The car park is monitored by CCTV so her car is safe. She uses a swipe card to get entry into the car park and then parks and walks into the office. She is being recorded by the CCTV system.

Figure 5 Lorna enters the staff car park

> **Q** What information might be stored on the swipe card? Why might some people not like the idea of being recorded on CCTV?

Lorna uses the same swipe card to get access to the office building that she works in. She sits in front of her computer ready to work. This isn't the first computer system that Lorna has come across today. In fact, she has already used several computer systems.

Figure 6 Lorna entering the office using a swipe card entry system

> **Q** What computer systems has Lorna used today? Has it been useful for Lorna to use these systems? Are there any possible problems with using computer systems like these?

5.1 Creating sets of instructions to control events

In this unit you will learn:
> **How computers are used to control events**
> **How to write efficient instructions to control events**
> **How to consider all possibilities in a control system**
> **How to create flowcharts from scratch**

Introduction

The purpose of this unit is for you to create a set of control instructions and a flowchart from scratch.

We might think of a computer as a tower or desktop unit, a keyboard, a mouse and a screen. In fact, computers are being used around us all the time. Computer microchips (chips) are used to control everything, from calculators to aeroplanes. Computers used in this way are sometimes called embedded computers, because the microchip is embedded inside another device.

All computers have one thing in common – they are basically stupid! This is because they will only do exactly what they are told to do. We tell them what to do by writing instructions.

 Written Task: Writing control instructions

In this task you will be asked to write instructions for a computer-controlled system. Open the 'Writing control instructions' worksheet on the website and follow the instructions.

Writing instructions

In InteraCT 1, we looked at how flowcharts are used to show how a control system might work. The first stage of writing a flowchart is to write down every step that is involved. For example, Figure 1 shows a digital photograph machine.

You find these in shops and they can be used to print digital photographs from a phone, camera or a CD. They work like this:

1 The user presses the touch screen to tell the machine whether they are using a phone, a memory card or a CD.
2 The user puts the memory card or CD into the machine.
3 If they are using their phone, it will use a wireless connection (such as Bluetooth).
4 The machine finds the photograph files and displays them on the screen.
5 The user selects which ones they want to print.
6 The user puts the correct money into the machine.
7 The machine prints the photographs.

This is the simple version. Because computers are stupid, you have to think about everything that could go wrong and make sure that you tell the computer what to do in each case. For example:

> What if the user selects the option to use a memory card and then tries to use their phone?
> What if the user does not put in the right amount of money?
> What if the machine runs out of paper?

In many cases, it might simply involve having suitable error messages on screen to tell the user they have done something wrong.

Creating the flowchart

The flowchart for the digital photograph machine might look like Figure 1.

Notice that there is a decision box toward the end that is used to check that the user has put the right amount of money in the machine.

Also notice that there is a loop being used. When the photographs have printed, the whole sequence starts again. It carries on like this until someone switches the machine off.

INPUT 1 is the touch screen. The user selects whether they are using a media card, mobile phone or CD

INPUT 2 is the memory card reader

The machine uploads the images onto its hard drive

INPUT 1 is the touch screen. The user is shown the photographs on screen and chooses the ones they want to print

INPUT 3 is the credit card reader. The user puts the card in

If there is a wrong amount there will be an error message displayed

OUPUT 2 is the printer. If it is the correct amount, the photographs will print. The process then starts again for the next user, and so on.

Figure 1 Flowchart for digital photograph machine

End of Unit Activity:

Creating a flowchart

In this activity you will be asked to create a flowchart. Open the 'Creating a flowchart' worksheet on the website and follow the instructions.

5.2 | Making control instructions more precise

In this unit you will learn:
> **How to create more precise instructions**
> **How control systems cope with real-life situations**

Introduction

Figure 1 Pedestrian crossing lights

When you create a set of instructions for a computer control system it is important to be as precise as possible. For example, to control the green man on a pedestrian crossing you could write these instructions:

1 User presses the button.
2 Wait.
3 Green man comes on.
4 Wait.
5 Green man goes off.

The instructions are not wrong, but this is not exactly what happens. Once a control system has been programmed to do something it will carry out the instructions it has been given over and over again. It is important therefore, that the instructions are as precise and accurate as possible.

Writing precise instructions

If we stick with the pedestrian crossing example, let's look at precisely what happens on a pedestrian crossing.

As you can see there are quite a few variables involved:

> The red man goes off when the green man comes on.
> The green man flashes before he goes off.
> The green man stays on for about 30 seconds.
> There is a WAIT sign that lights up above the button.

The flowchart in Figure 2 shows a much more precise set of instructions for controlling the pedestrian crossing.

Figure 2 Flowchart for
pedestrian crossing lights

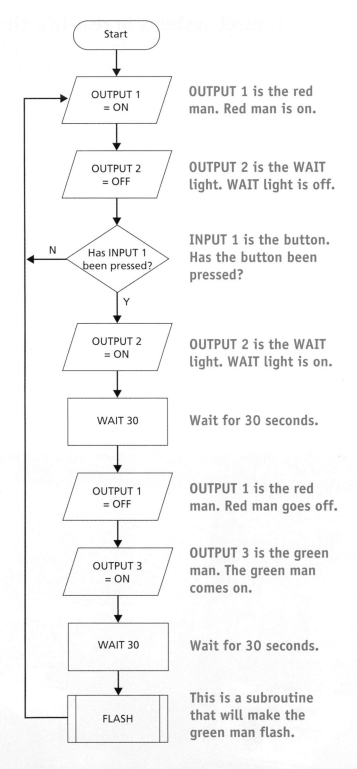

Start

OUTPUT 1
= ON

OUTPUT 1 is the red
man. Red man is on.

OUTPUT 2
= OFF

OUTPUT 2 is the WAIT
light. WAIT light is off.

Has INPUT 1
been pressed?   N

INPUT 1 is the button.
Has the button been
pressed?

Y

OUTPUT 2
= ON

OUTPUT 2 is the WAIT
light. WAIT light is on.

WAIT 30

Wait for 30 seconds.

OUTPUT 1
= OFF

OUTPUT 1 is the red
man. Red man goes off.

OUTPUT 3
= ON

OUTPUT 3 is the green
man. The green man
comes on.

WAIT 30

Wait for 30 seconds.

FLASH

This is a subroutine
that will make the
green man flash.

Written Task: Problems in control systems

**In this task you will be asked to identify problems in
a computer-controlled system. Open the 'Problems in
control systems' worksheet on the website and follow
the instructions.**

Control systems in real-life situations

Control systems have to take account of everything and anything that might happen in real life, for example:

> What happens with a car-park barrier if a car breaks down under it?
> What happens with a robotic lawnmower if a dog runs in front of it?
> What happens with a vending machine if someone puts the wrong money in?

Many control systems are used in dangerous situations, so the instructions have to be accurate. For example, control systems are used to land aeroplanes and to guide missiles. It would be serious if the person who programmed these systems got it wrong, or did not think of everything that might happen.

Take the pedestrian crossing as an example. In real life, some people are blind or partially sighted. Therefore, the control system must take account of this. The solution is to add sound with the green man so that blind people know when to cross. An extra output (OUTPUT 4) could be added to take account of this (see Figure 4).

Figure 3 Control system used to land an aeroplane

Figure 4 Flowchart for pedestrian crossing beeper

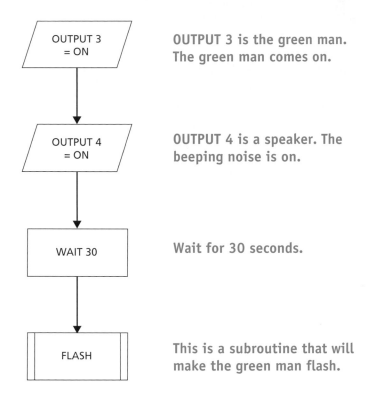

OUTPUT 3 = ON — **OUTPUT 3 is the green man. The green man comes on.**

OUTPUT 4 = ON — **OUTPUT 4 is a speaker. The beeping noise is on.**

WAIT 30 — **Wait for 30 seconds.**

FLASH — **This is a subroutine that will make the green man flash.**

Figure 5 Class photograph

End of Unit Activity: Photobooth
In this activity you will be asked to design a flowchart for a photo booth system. Open the 'Photobooth' worksheet on the website and follow the instructions.

5.3 | Making control instructions more efficient

In this unit you will learn how to:
> **Create more efficient instructions**
> **Use subroutines**
> **Use loops**
> **Use a counter**

Introduction

When you create a set of instructions for a computer control system you should try to be as efficient as possible. This means that you should try to write as few instructions as possible to make the system work.

Sometimes you might find that you are repeating the same instructions over and over again – this is inefficient. Sometimes you might find that there is a whole section of the flowchart that you can use again – this is efficient.

Repeated instructions

You could write these instructions to make the green man flash on a pedestrian crossing:

1 Green man on.
2 Wait 1 second.
3 Green man off.
4 Wait 1 second.
5 Green man on.
6 Wait 1 second.
7 Green man off.
8 Wait 1 second.

These instructions would make the green man flash twice. Notice that instructions 5 to 8 are exactly the same as instructions 1 to 4. These instructions are not wrong, but the green man should flash five or six times, so you would have to write out instructions 1 to 4 several times. This is inefficient.

To solve this problem, you need to put in a loop, as Figure 1 shows. Notice that the main instructions only need to be written once and then you can loop back to the start.

Written Task:
Writing efficient instructions

In this task you will be asked to write instructions as efficiently as possible. Open the 'Writing efficient instructions' worksheet on the website and follow the instructions.

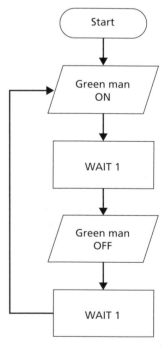

Figure 1 Flowchart for a loop in pedestrian crossing lights

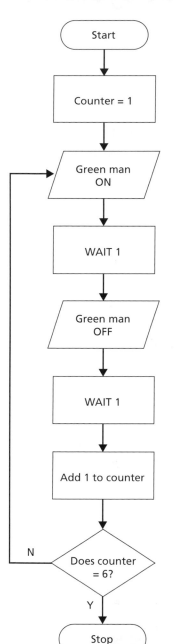

There is still a problem with this. We have not told the system how many times the green man should flash. This is where a counter can be used.

The flowchart in Figure 2 shows the four main instructions, but this time there is a counter used to count to 6. After the instructions have run through six times, the green man will stop flashing.

Repeating whole sections of the flowchart

Sometimes, you might need to use a whole section of a flowchart in more than one place on the flowchart. For example, in Figure 3, which is a flowchart for a burglar alarm system, there are two things that could set off the alarm:

> The burglar breaks in through the window.
> The burglar breaks in through the door.

In either case, the result is the same – the alarm goes off and the lights come on.

This is where a subroutine can be used. The instructions to set the alarm off and make the lights flash can be written once and saved as a subroutine. Then you can run the subroutine whenever it is needed.

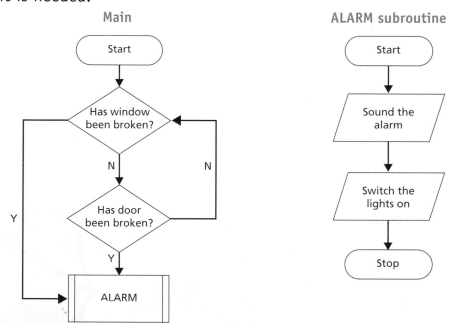

Figure 2 Flowchart for a loop that runs six times

Figure 3 Flowchart for a burglar alarm system

End of Unit Activity: Efficient flowcharts

In this activity you will be asked to design a flowchart as efficiently as possible. You may include a loop, subroutine and counter. Open the 'Efficient flowcharts' worksheet on the website and follow the instructions.

5.4 | Monitoring and control systems

In this unit you will learn:
> How control systems are used in everyday life
> What monitoring is and how it links with control
> The advantages and disadvantages of using control systems
> Why some people are worried about the use of monitoring and control systems

Introduction

The use of computers to control devices and events is becoming more and more common. Computers now control many household items. For example, your MP3 player, CD and DVD systems, your television, microwave oven, phone and even your fridge all have a computer chip in them.

Computer control is also used a lot by large organisations. For example, the National Health Service uses health monitoring and control systems to diagnose illnesses and keep people alive. All commercial airlines now use computer control systems to fly and even land their planes.

Monitoring

Monitoring means 'to keep a check on'. Many control systems also include monitoring. For example:

> The police use speed cameras to monitor vehicle speeds.
> Hospitals use heart-rate monitors on critically ill patients.

The purpose of monitoring is so that the control system can act if there is a problem:

> The speed camera takes a picture if a vehicle is going too fast.
> The heart-rate monitor sounds an alarm if the heart rate becomes dangerous.

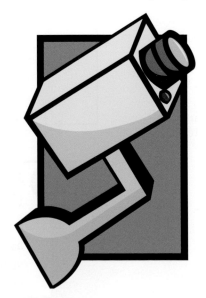

Figure 1 Monitoring system

Figure 2 Heart-rate monitor

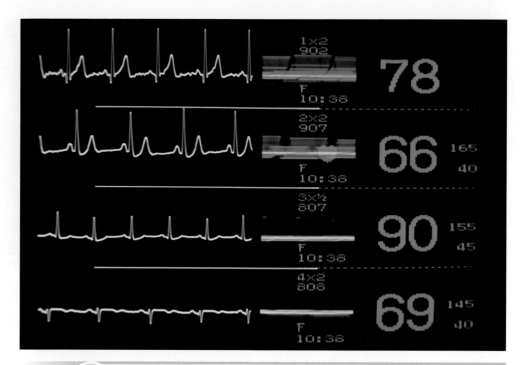

Written Task: Monitoring and control systems

In this task you will be asked to identify what different monitoring and control systems do. Open the 'Monitoring and control systems' worksheet on the website and follow the instructions.

The advantages of control systems

In most cases, control systems are a great advantage to us and to society as a whole. In some cases, computer control just makes our life easier:

> We can leave our food to cook in a microwave oven without having to keep an eye on it.
> We don't have to open doors ourselves, as they open automatically.
> We can record television programmes when we are out and watch them later.

In some cases, the control system might make us safer or even save our lives:

> Nuclear power stations can operate safely without over-heating.
> Airbags can save people's lives if there is a car crash.
> The electricity in a house cuts off automatically if someone accidentally cuts though a power cable.

Figure 3 Airbags

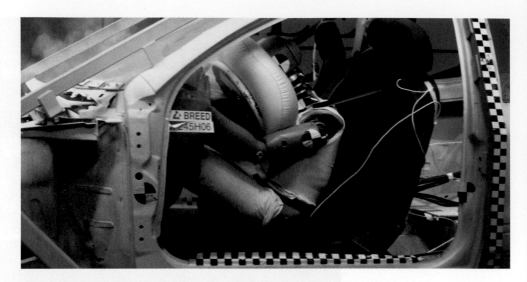

Disadvantages of control systems

In some cases, computer control can be a disadvantage. What happens when the system fails? In most cases, it might just be frustrating. For example:

> The food in the microwave is over- or under-cooked.
> The automatic door doesn't open.
> The DVD recorder records the wrong programme.

In more serious cases, if the system fails, people's health or lives could be at risk:

> The nuclear power station could overheat and explode.
> The airbags on the car do not inflate.
> The electricity does not cut off.

Figure 4 When a system fails

Big Brother

Some people are worried that computers are being used to monitor and control our everyday lives. They think that we are being watched all the time:

> When people go into town, they might be recorded on CCTV systems (Figure 5).
> When someone uses a mobile phone, their location can be recorded.
> In some schools, when pupils take a book out of the library or buy a school meal, they have their fingerprints checked.

Figure 5 CCTV camera

 End of Unit Activity: Is Big Brother watching you?

In this activity you will be asked your opinion on the use of computer systems to monitor people. Open the 'Is Big Brother watching you?' worksheet on the website and follow the instructions.

 End of Module Assignment: Controlling a toll booth

In this assignment you will be asked to create a flowchart to control the toll booths on a toll road. Open the 'Module 5 assignment' worksheet on the website and follow the instructions.

Case Study introduction

Figure 1 The Farhan family

Figure 1 shows the Farhan family. Grandad Farid and Grandma Dalali are retired now. Maalik Farhan is a bank manager and his wife Wendy is a dentist. They have two children. Carmel is 19. She is studying sociology at college. Jamie is the youngest. He's in Year 8.

> **Q** How do you think each member of the family might use ICT? Why might there be differences in what they each use ICT for?

It's breakfast time in the Farhan house. Maalik is opening the post. He has got three letters asking him if he wants a new credit card. Maalik calls this junk mail. He has also got a surprise from his bank. They are asking him to repay a loan for £10,000. Maalik has never taken out a loan. He's confused.

> **Q** Why might Maalik gets lots of junk mail? Where did the credit card companies get his name and address from? Why do you think the bank is asking Maalik to repay money that he has not even spent?

Figure 2 The Farhan family at breakfast

The Farhan family keep the family computer in the dining room. They all use the computer quite a lot, but Jamie uses it the most. He uses it whenever he can. He usually goes on the computer for a few minutes before he has to set off for school. He sometimes has his meals sitting at the computer and he will use it late into the evening as well. His mum Wendy always gets annoyed about this.

Figure 3 Jamie sitting at the computer desk

> **Q** What health and safety problems might there be with what Jamie is doing? What would you do to make the computer area a bit safer and more comfortable?

It's 4.30 p.m. and Jamie is back on the computer. This time he is using the Internet to do his homework. His art teacher wants him to find out some information about the painter Mondrian. He finds some useful information and copies and pastes it into Word. He adds several pictures he has found using an image search. He prints it off and puts it in his bag. He can now get on with downloading some new songs to his MP3 player.

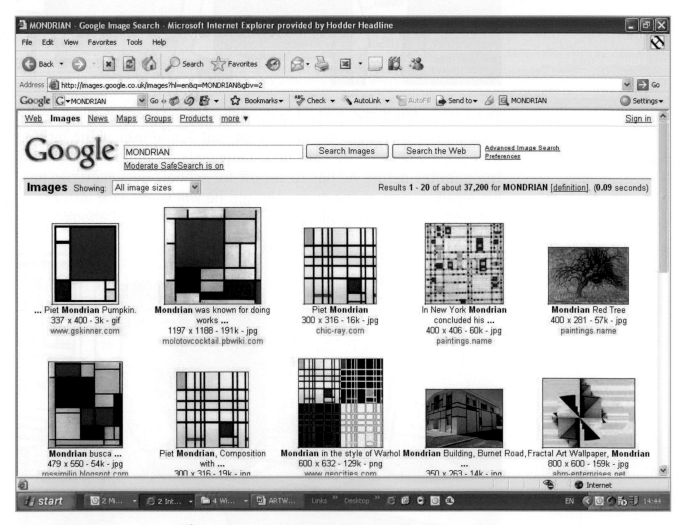

Figure 4 Results of an image search on the painter Mondrian

Figure 5 Jamie downloading songs from the Internet

> **Q** Why might what Jamie has just done be wrong? Why might it be illegal? How could Jamie make sure that he does not do anything wrong or illegal when getting information, images and music from the Internet?

Another day in the Farhan household and the whole family is having breakfast together – even Jamie. Maalik is opening the post as usual and moaning as usual about the amount of junk mail he has got. There is a letter for Carmel. She has just found out that she has got a job with a homeless charity when she finishes her course. As part of her course, she has studied the different types of social problems faced by people all over the world.

> **Q** Why might some people in the UK not have access to ICT? Why might some people in other countries not have access to ICT? What could be done to help these people get access to ICT?

6.1 Misuse of personal data

In this unit you will learn:
> **What personal data are**
> **How personal data might be misused**
> **What laws protect your personal data**
> **What you can do to protect your personal data**

Figure 1 Who can see your data?

Personal data

What are personal data?

Personal data are any information that identifies a living person. Basically, this means that any data that include your full name are personal data. For example, your doctor and your school are just two examples of organisations that store your personal data.

These people store your personal data because they need it for their jobs. However, some information is sensitive and you might not want everyone to know about it. For example:

> Medical information held by your doctor. It is useful for your doctor to have it, but you wouldn't want him or her to share it with anybody else.
> The information and grades written on your Year 8 report. The school, teachers and parents need to see it, but you might not want your friends to.

How data can be misused

Once another person or organisation has your personal details they could misuse them. This means that they could use them for a purpose that they are not supposed to be used for. For example, you might give your doctor personal details about your health. The doctor might then sell your medical details to a drugs company who might use them to try to sell you their brand of drugs.

A more serious example is if someone gets hold of your personal data and then pretends to be you. This is called **identity theft**. The people who do this usually do it so that they can steal money from your bank account, or order things on the Internet using your details. They could also commit other crimes, which might then get linked back to you because they are using your name and personal details.

Written Task: Misuse of data

In this task you will be asked to think about the ways that personal data might be misused. Open the 'Misuse of data' worksheet on the website and follow the instructions.

Figure 2 Some personal data you might not want everyone to know

Personal data and the law

The Government introduced a law called the **Data Protection Act**. The idea of it is to stop people or organisations misusing your data. Like all laws, it is complicated, but the basics of it are that anyone who wants to store your personal details must be registered with a government official called the Data Protection Commissioner. Once they are registered they must:

> Only use the data for the reason they said they would use them.
> Keep the data safe and secure.
> Make sure the data are correct and up to date.
> Not give or sell the data to anyone else without your permission.

Protecting your personal data

You have a legal right to know what information people hold about you. For example, you are allowed to ask your doctor, or your school to show you your personal information. If you think someone has some information about you that is wrong, you can ask them to put it right and they must do this.

You can also protect your personal data to try to stop people getting hold of them in the first place. Every time you register with a website or fill in a form, or enter a competition, your personal details are being stored on a database somewhere. You should think twice about who you give your personal information to.

There are lots of people who try to get hold of your personal data without you even knowing about it. Every time you are online, your personal data could be collected. This might be done through spyware software, which installs itself on your computer and automatically records information that you type into websites. You might also be asked for your personal details in an email. These emails look like they are from a bank and they ask you for your bank details.

There are some things you can do to protect your data:

> Use anti-virus and spyware removal software.
> Use a firewall to stop hackers.
> Use passwords on your system and on your important files.
> Never give your personal details to anyone unless you are sure you know who they are.

Figure 3 Protect your data from unauthorised users

 End of Unit Activity: Keeping personal data safe

In this activity you will be asked to consider how you can keep your personal data safe. Open the 'Keeping personal data safe' worksheet on the website and follow the instructions.

6.2 Health and safety issues

In this unit you will learn:
> What health and safety is
> About physical injuries and how to avoid them
> About strains and how to avoid them
> About stress and how to avoid it

What are health and safety issues?

Health and safety issues involve all the things that can cause you physical injury or mental stress. Anyone using a computer, especially if they use it a lot, should be aware of possible problems and take steps to avoid them. This covers the use of all types of computers, including games consoles.

In serious cases, you could be badly injured. For example, if you spill a drink over your computer you could get an electric shock. Some problems are less serious, such as headaches or eyestrain from using the computer too much.

Figure 1 Use your computer safely!

Avoiding physical injury

The two main threats here are:

Figure 2 Computer cables can cause danger of tripping

> Electrical safety – you are probably not allowed to bring drinks into the IT room at school. This is because fluids and electricity are dangerous when mixed. You might also notice little stickers on all the electrical equipment in your school. This is to show that the equipment has been checked and is safe to use. When you are at home, make sure that you do not plug too many things into the same socket.
> Tripping – computers need lots of cables and when cables are left dangling they can be dangerous. Most computer rooms have the cables hidden in the walls or under the floor rather than leaving them trailing across the floor where someone could trip over them.

Avoiding strains

Whenever you carry out repetitive physical tasks, you run the risk of straining something. This is called **repetitive strain injury** (RSI). The types of strain you might get when using a computer are:

> eye strain and headaches from staring at the screen
> arm, hand, wrist or finger strain from using the keyboard, mouse, joystick or controller
> shoulder and back strain from sitting in the same position for too long.

To avoid strains:

> Take regular breaks away from the computer.
> Adjust the position of the screen so that there is no glare.
> Set the brightness to reduce the amount of glare.
> Adjust your sitting position so that you are comfortable.
> Angle the keyboard rather than using it flat.
> Use foot and wrist rests.
> Make sure the room you are working in has the right heating and lighting and is not too noisy – not always easy when you are at school!
> Get rid of all the clutter around your computer so you have got room to work.

Figure 3 shows the ideal position for you and your computer equipment:

Figure 3 Sit correctly to avoid strain

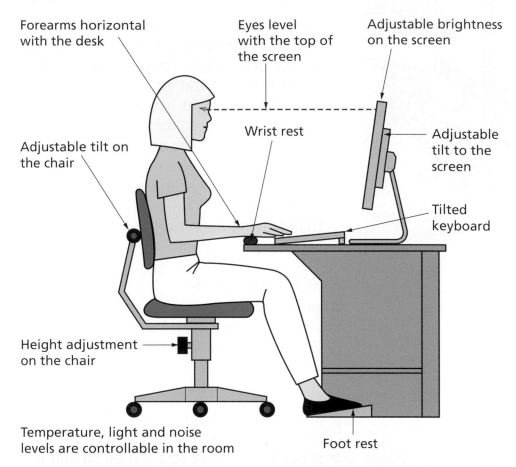

Forearms horizontal with the desk

Eyes level with the top of the screen

Adjustable brightness on the screen

Adjustable tilt on the chair

Wrist rest

Adjustable tilt to the screen

Tilted keyboard

Height adjustment on the chair

Temperature, light and noise levels are controllable in the room

Foot rest

Figure 4 Be careful not to overload sockets!

Figure 5 Fluids and electricity are dangerous when mixed!

Stress

Stress is when you are feeling anxious or under pressure. A bit of stress can be a good thing as it helps you to get your work done on time, but too much stress can make you feel tired, irritable or even ill.

Stress can be caused when you have lots of work to do or if someone is putting pressure on you.

You can avoid stress by:

> writing out a plan (or list) of everything that needs doing
> taking regular short breaks away from the computer
> showing respect in the way you deal with other people, including when you are online.

 Written Task: Health and safety policy

In this task you will be asked to write a health and safety policy for your school. Open the 'Health and safety policy' worksheet on the website and follow the instructions.

 End of Unit Activity: Health and safety and you

In this activity you will be asked to think about the health and safety issues related to using ICT. Open the 'Health and safety and you' worksheet on the website and follow the instructions.

6.3 | Plagiarism and copyright

Learning Objectives	**In this unit you will learn:**
	> **What plagiarism is**
	> **How to avoid plagiarism**
	> **What copyright is**
	> **What is covered by copyright**

Introduction

As a pupil you probably use ICT a lot. This might include using the Internet to do your homework, watching videos over the Internet or downloading music and games onto your computer. Whenever you do any of these things you have to make sure that you don't **plagiarise** and that you don't break the law on **copyright**.

Figure 1 Don't plagiarise!

Plagiarism

Plagiarism is when you copy someone else's work and claim that you did it yourself. This is not a new problem but, because we all use the Internet so much now, it has become a bigger problem.

For example, if a pupil was given some homework about volcanoes it would be easy for them to do a quick search on the Internet, find a good site and then copy and paste whole blocks of text into a document. The pupil could add a title and their name and they would have done their homework in about two minutes.

The problem with this is:

> It's cheating. Some people see it as stealing.
> It could be illegal.
> The pupil doesn't learn anything.
> The pupil could get into serious trouble.

Plagiarism is a problem in schools and colleges, but it doesn't stop there. For example:

> Writers often accuse other writers of plagiarising their stories.
> Scientists accuse other scientists of plagiarising their research.
> Software companies accuse others of stealing their ideas for programs.

In some cases, people sue each other for millions of pounds if they think someone has stolen their work.

You are allowed to use other people's work for research reasons, but you cannot just copy it word for word. If you are caught plagiarising work in your GCSE coursework for example, you may not be allowed to sit any of your GCSE exams.

When you use someone else's work for research, you need to:

> use more than one source
> put it into your own words
> state where you got the information from.

 Written Task: Plagiarism

In this task you will be asked to think about plagiarism. Open the 'Plagiarism' worksheet on the website and follow the instructions.

Copyright

Copyright is the law that stops people from stealing other people's work. You might create an original piece of work, which might be a story, a play, a movie, a photograph or a song. You then 'own the copyright' on this work. This means that no one else can use it unless they have asked for your permission.

You might come across copyright when you download things from the Internet. Copyright covers books, music tracks, music videos, photographs, films, television programmes and software (including games). Some people do give their work away for free, but you usually have to pay for legal downloads.

Most of the money goes to the person who created the work in the first place. Copyright is used to make sure that people get the credit for the work they have done and this includes getting paid for it.

If you download illegally, you are breaking the copyright law and you can get a large fine if you are caught.

 End of Unit Activity: Copyright and you

In this activity you will be asked to think about copyright and how it affects you. Open the 'Copyright and you' worksheet on the website and follow the instructions.

6.4

The impact of ICT

Learning Objectives

In this unit you will learn:
> **How ICT affects employment**
> **How some people might not have access to ICT**
> **How ICT is used across the world**

Introduction

ICT has become an important part of modern life. ICT is used in the home, at school and at work. ICT is used so much that it has had an impact on our society. In some ways, ICT makes people's lives better and in some ways it can make them worse. There are also some parts of society who do not have access to ICT at all.

Employment

According to the Government, around 95% of people of working age in this country have jobs. ICT is used more and more in the workplace and it has created many jobs. However, some people's jobs have changed because of ICT and some have even lost their jobs. There have been some winners and some losers.

Winners
> Floyd is a web designer. He creates and looks after websites for businesses.
> Carl is a computer technician. He works in a large computer store where he builds and fixes computers.
> Clare is a journalist. She works from home and sends her articles in electronically.

Losers
> Mia worked in a bank. Her branch was closed down as more people were doing their banking online or over the phone.
> Andy worked in a car factory. He was made redundant and replaced by a robot.
> Shuili used to run a music shop. The shop had to close because people were buying music online or downloading instead of using her shop.

Figure 1 Carl the computer technician

Figure 2 Andy used to work in a car factory

Access to ICT

Some people are worried about what they call the **digital divide**. This means that although there are lots of people who do benefit from ICT, there are some people who cannot get access to ICT.

Figure 3 There is not always a digital divide between the old and young

This might be because they have not had access to education, they may be poor or old, or there may be religious reasons that prevent them from using ICT.

If they cannot get access to ICT they may be at a disadvantage. For example:

> Many people have no ICT training and they might find it difficult to get a job with no ICT skills.
> Lots of help, advice and information is available over the Internet. The people that need this help the most might not get it because they don't have access to the Internet in the first place.

ICT across the world

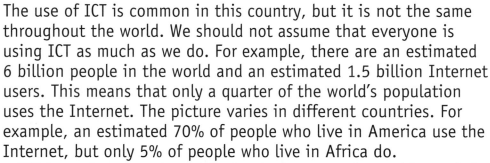

The use of ICT is common in this country, but it is not the same throughout the world. We should not assume that everyone is using ICT as much as we do. For example, there are an estimated 6 billion people in the world and an estimated 1.5 billion Internet users. This means that only a quarter of the world's population uses the Internet. The picture varies in different countries. For example, an estimated 70% of people who live in America use the Internet, but only 5% of people who live in Africa do.

ICT is used more and more in developing countries and it can help them to become richer. For example, people in developing countries:

Figure 4 Access to ICT is more difficult in developing countries

> can use the Internet to find customers for their products all over the world
> can use new technology to improve their education and health services
> can develop new technology to produce the food and other products they need more efficiently.

Written Task: ICT in developing countries

In this task you will be asked to think about how ICT could be used in developing countries. Open the 'ICT in developing countries' worksheet on the website and follow the instructions.

End of Unit Activity: The impact of ICT

In this activity you will be asked how you think ICT affects people's lives. Open the 'The impact of ICT' worksheet on the website and follow the instructions.

 End of Module Assignment: Keeping an ICT diary

In this assignment you will be asked to keep a diary of how you use ICT. You will then compare your use of ICT to other people's. Open the 'Module 6 assignment' worksheet on the website and follow the instructions.

7 INTEGRATED TASKS

In this book we have looked at lots of different uses of ICT. We have covered:

> **Finding information:** using the Internet and other sources
> **Presenting information:** using word-processing, desktop publishing, presentation and website creation software
> **Modelling:** using spreadsheets
> **Data handling:** using databases
> **Control:** using flowcharts.

So far we have looked at each of these things separately. In real life, a combination of ICT software and tools are usually used to complete a task. For example, if someone was running a shop they might:

> Use desktop-publishing software to create adverts and posters.
> Use word-processing software to write letters to customers and suppliers.
> Use web-design software to make a website.
> Use spreadsheets to look after the finances and work out the wages.
> Use databases to store information about the products they sell and how much they cost.

It is also quite likely that the shop might 'integrate' the use of software. This means that they might move data and information from one piece of software to another. For example:

> They might use the information stored on the database to update the information about prices on their website.
> They might use product information and photographs on their website to create an advert using DTP software.

There are three integrated tasks on the website for you to complete:

1 'The catalogue shop' covers data handling, presentation and control.
2 'Choose and Book' covers data handling, presentation and web design.
3 'Predicting the weather' covers monitoring and modelling.

The idea of these tasks is that you use the software and tools that you think are needed to carry out the tasks. You should use the skills and knowledge that you have gained during this course to complete the tasks as well as you can.

Producing an e-portfolio

The integrated tasks require you to complete a number of assignments. It is important that you create a suitable folder and file structure to store all of this work.

You create an electronic portfolio, which is a collection of files and folders stored in your area. Your teacher may choose to mark them on the computer rather than asking you to print them out. Therefore, it is important that the files have sensible and meaningful names and that they are organised into suitable folders that make it clear what is in the folder.

Figure 1 Different uses of ICT explored in the Integrated Tasks module

7.1 | The catalogue shop

Learning Objectives	In this unit you use a range of ICT skills and knowledge to:
	> **Create a page of a catalogue using appropriate information and images**
	> **Create a flowchart to control a self-service kiosk**
	> **Create a 'user interface' for the computer systems used in the shop**

Introduction

Figure 1 Keypad used to check the stock

Catalogue shops work by having an area where customers come in and can browse through a catalogue that contains thousands of items. The catalogue is organised into categories so that similar items are in the same place. Each page might contain information on several different products.

Every item has:

> a colour photograph
> a brief description
> the price
> a catalogue number.

Selecting and buying the item

The first part of the process is for the customer to find the item they want to buy, check it is in stock, order it and pay for it:

1 The customer browses through the catalogue and finds what they want.
2 They type the catalogue number into a keypad.
3 This checks the stock database to see if the item is available.
4 If the item is in stock, the customer writes the number on a form and gives it to the cashier.
5 They could use a **self-service kiosk** and pay automatically by credit card.
6 Either way, a receipt is printed with an order number and a collection point on it.

 Integrated Task: Designing a page of the catalogue

In this task you will be asked to create a page of a catalogue. Open the 'Designing a page of the catalogue' worksheet on the website and follow the instructions.

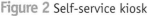

Figure 2 Self-service kiosk

Integrated Task: Controlling the self-service kiosk

In this task you will be asked to create a flowchart to control a self-service kiosk. Open the 'Controlling the self-service kiosk' worksheet on the website and follow the instructions.

Getting the item from the warehouse

The second part is that while the customer waits in the shop, one of the workers has to fetch the product from the warehouse out the back:

1 The order is displayed on a screen in the warehouse.
2 One of the workers checks the catalogue number and then goes and finds the product.
3 When they have found it they take it up to the counter for the customer to collect.
4 The barcode on the item is scanned and recorded in the stock database.

Keeping the customer informed

It might take a few minutes for the item to be found and brought to the counter. Although the customer is waiting:

1 A visual display shows what order number is now being processed.
2 It also shows which order numbers are in the queue.
3 When the item is ready at the collection point, it will flash up the order number of that product.

Integrated Task: Screen designs

In this task you will be asked to create a 'user interface' for the computer systems used in the shop. Open the 'Screen designs' worksheet on the website and follow the instructions.

7.2

Choose and Book

In this unit you use a range of ICT skills and knowledge to:
> **Design a suitable structure for a database**
> **Examine a database**
> **Create a web page or website**

Figure 1 A GP surgery

Introduction

When someone gets ill, they normally go to their GP. If the GP thinks that they need further treatment, the GP will arrange an appointment at a hospital. This can sometimes take several days or even weeks.

The new 'Choose and Book' system is being introduced to let GPs make hospital appointments for their patients instantly.

The old system

The old system worked like this:

1 The patient goes to see their GP.
2 The GP says that they need hospital treatment, e.g., an X-ray.
3 The GP writes to the hospital asking for an appointment.
4 The hospital writes back to the patient telling them when and where the appointment is.

There have been problems with this system:

> Patients have to wait several days or even weeks to find out when and where the appointment is.
> The appointment might be inconvenient for the patient. Perhaps they cannot get to that hospital at the stated time.
> If the appointment is inconvenient, the patient has to contact the hospital to get another appointment.

The new system

The new system will work like this:

1 The patient goes to see their GP.
2 The GP says that they need hospital treatment, e.g., an X-ray.
3 The GP logs onto the 'Choose and Book' system while the patient is with them.
4 They pick a hospital and a time that is convenient for the patient and the booking is made there and then.
5 The GP prints off the details and hands them to the patient.

How it works

There are two main parts to this system:

> A *database* that contains patient details, details of all the hospitals in the area, what services they offer and what appointment times they have.
> A *website* that the GPs can log onto that includes an online booking form.

Some GPs are worried about the new 'Choose and Book' system. They think that patients might complain if they try to book an appointment but find that the hospital they want to go to does not have any free appointments. Some hospitals are more popular than others and some appointment times are more popular than others.

 Integrated Task: GP database

In this task you will be asked to design and examine a database. Open the 'GP database' worksheet on the website and follow the instructions.

Figure 2 Home page of the Choose and Book website

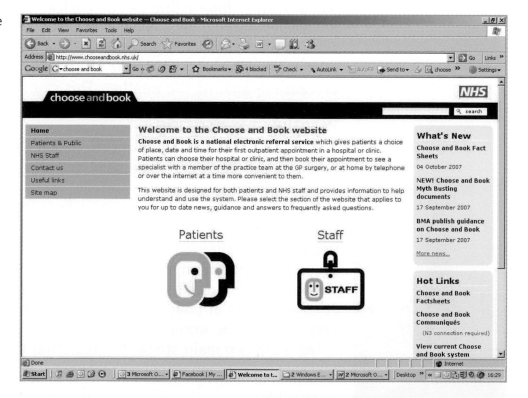

 Integrated Task: Choose and Book website

In this task you will be asked to create a web page or website. Open the 'Choose and Book website' worksheet on the website and follow the instructions.

7.3 Predicting the weather

Learning Objectives   **In this unit you use a range of ICT skills and knowledge to:**
> **Carry out research using the Internet**
> **Create one or more presentation**
> **Use and update a model to make predictions**

Introduction

People have always tried to predict the weather for many reasons. For example, weather forecasts:

> Are vital for people who work at sea, such as fishermen, ferry owners and oil-refinery workers.
> Are important for people who work outdoors or on the land, such as farmers.
> Are useful for members of the general public.

Some weather forecasting can be critical. For example, scientists are always working on ways of predicting serious weather events such as tornadoes and hurricanes. If the public are given a warning that serious weather is on the way, they can take precautions against the weather. This can save thousands of lives.

Weather forecasting

In the UK, the Meteorological Office (Met Office) has been predicting the weather since 1854 and since 1962 they have been using computers.

Predicting the weather is complicated. It requires masses of data and enormous computing power. In fact, the computers they use are called **supercomputers** because they have lots of processing power and storage.

Figure 2 shows the NEC supercomputer that the Met Office uses. It cost millions of pounds and is one of the most powerful computers in the world.

There are two main stages to predicting the weather:

1 Collect as many weather data from as many different places as possible.
2 Enter these data into a computer model and use them to predict what will happen.

Figure 1 Weather station

Figure 2 The Met Office supercomputer

 Integrated Task: Hurricane research

In this task you will be asked to carry out some research on hurricanes using the Internet and also create one or more presentations. Open the 'Hurricane research' worksheet on the website and follow the instructions.

Modelling the weather

A model is when real-life situations are created on a computer. They let you ask 'what if?' questions:

> What if there are high winds out at sea?
> What if the temperature of the sea is high?
> What if the air is humid?

The Met Office models are complicated. This is because there are so many different things that might happen that will affect the weather.

We are going to recreate a simpler version of the kind of thing that the Met Office does with a spreadsheet model. Again, we concentrate on hurricanes and how to predict when one is coming.

 Integrated Task: Hurricane model

In this task you will be asked to use and update a model to make predictions. Open the 'Hurricane model' worksheet on the website and follow the instructions.

KEYWORDS GLOSSARY

Unit	Keyword	Definition
1.1	Fact	A statement that can be checked to see whether it is true
1.1	Opinion	A statement that reflects what someone thinks about something
1.1	Reliable	Refers to information and whether it can be trusted to be correct
1.1	URL	The address of a website
1.2	Bias	Refers to information that is presented from one particular point of view
1.2	Up-to-date	Refers to information that is current. It is the latest information available
1.2	Validity	Refers to information in terms of whether it is true or not. Valid information is information that you believe to be true
1.3	Hits	The list of web pages that are shown after a search
1.3	Keywords	The words that you type into a search engine to help you find relevant information
1.3	Links	One web page is connected to another with a link
1.3	Rank	The order that the results are put into after a search
1.3	Results	The list of web pages that are shown after a search
1.3	Search engine	A website that searches the Internet based on keywords
1.3	Sponsored links	When the owner of a website pays a search engine to put their site at the top of the results page
1.4	Console	A type of computer display
1.4	Hyperlink	A way of connecting one page or slide to another by clicking
1.4	Interactive presentation	A slideshow where the user can decide which slides they want to look at
1.4	Menu bar	A list of options, usually positioned in the same place on every page
1.4	Presentation	Any method where information is shown to people - usually associated with slideshows
1.4	Slideshow	A series of slides
1.5	Balanced	Refers to information that shows all sides of an argument
1.5	Interview	A way of gathering information by asking people questions
1.5	News reporting	Information gathered and presented to people about current affairs
1.5	Script	A written version of something that will be read out
1.5	Sound recording software	Programs that are used to record sound
1.5	Specialist software	Programs that have a specific function
2.1	Clarity	Refers to the design of a website in terms of whether it is clear and easy to follow
2.1	Design	The process of working out how something is going to look and work, e.g. a website
2.1	Navigate	The way in which someone moves around a website
2.1	Navigation	The process of moving between pages in a website
2.1	Tab	Something you click on in a web page to link to other pages
2.1	Thumbnail	A small picture
2.1	Upload	The process of putting information onto a website
2.1	Web page	One page of information on a website

2.1	Website	A collection of web pages
2.2	Browser	Software used to view web pages, e.g. Internet Explorer
2.2	Code	Instructions that are typed into the computer
2.2	HTML	Stands for HyperText Mark-up Language and is a code used by a browser so that it knows how to display web pages
2.2	HTML format	Any file that can be displayed as a web page in a browser
2.2	Mark-up language	A way of writing instructions that will show how web pages should be displayed
2.2	Specialist software	Software that has a specific purpose, e.g. web design
2.2	Standard software	Software that has a general purpose, e.g. word processing or desktop publishing
2.3	Browser	Software used for viewing web pages
2.3	Internet Explorer	Microsoft's version of a browser
2.3	Mozilla	Browser software available for free from the Internet
2.3	Notepad	Microsoft's version of a text editor
2.3	Tags	Used in html code, e.g. <p> </p>
2.3	Text editor	Software used for typing in text
2.4	Button	A shape (usually with a text label) that you can add a hyperlink to
2.4	Styles	Settings for font style, size, position and colour
2.4	Themes	Formatting options that are applied to all pages
2.4	Website structure	The way in which all of the web pages link together in a website
2.5	Application form	A form that you fill in when applying for something, e.g. registering with a website
2.5	Linear	A type of website structure where one page follows another in a set sequence
2.5	Online form	A form that you fill in online
2.5	Online shopping	Buying things using the Internet
2.5	Random	A type of website structure where any page can be accessed from any other page
2.5	Tabs	A way of switching between pages on a website
2.5	Tree	A type of website structure where the pages are organised like a family tree
2.5	Website section	A group of web pages within a larger website
2.5	Wizard	Where you are taken through a process step by step
3.1	Predictions	Using a model to estimate what might happen in the future
3.1	Rules	In spreadsheet models, these are the way that formulae are used
3.1	Variables	In spreadsheet models, these are values that you can change as you use the model
3.1	What if	Asking questions by typing values into a spreadsheet model to see what effect it has
3.2	Accurate	In spreadsheet models, this is whether the values and results are correct or not
3.2	Drop-down lists	Cells that contain a list of options (accessed by clicking on a small arrow)
3.2	If statements	A type of formula that puts different values in a cell depending on the value in another cell

3.2	Realistic	In spreadsheet models, this is whether the model recreates real life accurately
3.3	Absolute cell reference	Used when setting up a spreadsheet formula to fix the cell reference, e.g. B1
3.3	Relative cell reference	The standard way of setting up a spreadsheet formula so that it automatically changes if you copy it into another cell
3.3	Table	A way of presenting data as columns and rows
3.3	Text labels	Text that is used on graphs to indicate what is being plotted on each axis
3.4	Investment	When you put money into something with the hope of getting more money out than you put in
3.4	Real-life	Refers to computer models and simulations that are based on things that happen in the real world
3.4	Simulation	A computer-based prediction of what might happen in real life
3.4	Variables	In spreadsheet models, these are values that you can change as you use the model
3.5	Conditional formatting	In a spreadsheet, the format of a cell changes automatically if certain values appear in the cell
3.5	Nested If statement	Several If statements joined together
3.5	RANDBETWEEN	A function in Excel that generates a random number between two numbers, e.g. RANDBETWEEN (1,6) generates a random number between 1 and 6
3.5	Random numbers	Numbers generated automatically in a spreadsheet that are completely random
4.1	Database software	Programs designed specifically for handling data
4.1	Data capture	Data that are collected automatically
4.1	Data collection	Data that are collected from a questionnaire or form
4.1	Data structure	The way that data are formatted and stored in a database
4.1	Field length	How much space is allowed for typing data into a database (see also Field size)
4.1	Field size	How much space is allowed for typing data into a database (see also Field length)
4.1	Form	Used in a database as a user-friendly way to enter and view records
4.1	Online form	A form that is available on a website
4.1	Police National Computer database	Stores information on criminals and crimes
4.1	Query	A search carried out in a database
4.1	Table	Used in a database to set up the data structure and view the data
4.2	Drop-down lists	Boxes on forms that contain a list of options
4.2	Computer-based forms	A way of collecting information on the computer
4.2	Online forms	A way of collecting information using a website
4.2	Paper-based forms	A way of collecting information by hand
4.2	Tick boxes	Boxes on forms that you can tick
4.2	User-friendly	Computer programs that are easy to use – they are designed with the user in mind
4.3	BETWEEN	Used when creating a query to search for values between two numbers

4.3	Complex query	A search using more than one criterion
4.3	Criteria	The plural of criterion
4.3	Criterion	The basis on which you are carrying out a query
4.3	Greater than	Used when creating a query to search for a value above a certain number
4.3	Greater than or equal to	Used when creating a query to search for a value that is the same as or above a certain number
4.3	Less than	Used when creating a query to search for a value below a certain number
4.3	Less than or equal to	Used when creating a query to search for a value that is the same as or below a certain number
4.3	Query	A search carried out in a database
4.3	Simple query	A search using one criterion
4.4	Columnar	A way of laying out a report in columns
4.4	Integrated	The idea of using data in one program and putting them into another program
4.4	Integrating	The process of taking data from one program and putting them into another program
4.4	Report	A way of presenting information in a database
4.4	Report heading	The title that appears at the top of the report
4.4	Tabular	A way of laying out a report in a table format, i.e. columns and rows
5.1	Bluetooth	One type of wireless connection. Used on many mobile phones
5.1	Chip	The short name for a computer microchip
5.1	Computer microchip	The processor that carries out all of the instructions
5.1	Error messages	Instructions that are displayed in a computer system when something goes wrong
5.1	Memory card	A device that stores data, e.g. stores pictures in a digital camera
5.1	Wireless connection	A way of sending data from one device to another without wires
5.2	Precision	How accurate or exact something is. In control, it means that the instructions are accurate and exact
5.2	Program	A set of instructions used to control a computer
5.2	Programmed	A computer system that is following instructions
5.2	Real-life situations	Anything that can happen for real as opposed to in a computer environment
5.2	Subroutine	A small section of a larger flowchart
5.3	Counter	A way of keeping count of something in a flowchart, e.g. how many times a light has flashed
5.3	Efficient instructions	In control, this is using as few instructions as possible to make the system work
5.3	Inefficient instructions	In control, this is when the system works, but lots of the instructions are repeated
5.3	Loop	A section of a flowchart that keeps repeating itself
5.3	Subroutine	A section of a flowchart that can be used over and over again
5.4	Big Brother	A term that means that someone (usually the Government) is watching you all the time
5.4	Control system	A computer system used to control a device or event

5.4	Monitoring	Keeping a check on something. Control systems include monitoring to keep a check on what it is controlling
5.4	Monitoring and Control system	A control system that includes monitoring. It checks on what it is controlling and then takes the necessary action
5.4	System failure	When a computer system breaks down or stops working properly
6.1	Anti-phishing software	Software that checks for emails from false banks
6.1	Data misuse	When data are used for a reason that they were not intended for
6.1	Data Protection Act	The law that tells people and organisations what they are allowed to do with personal data
6.1	Data Protection Registrar	A government official who is in charge of making sure that everyone sticks to the Data Protection Act
6.1	Firewall	A way of stopping hackers getting into your computer
6.1	Identity (ID) theft	When someone steals your personal information and pretends to be you
6.1	Password	A way of protecting your computer system and your files
6.1	Personal data/ information	Any information that identifies a living individual
6.1	Phishing	A way that criminals try to get your personal details by sending emails that look like they are from a bank
6.1	Sensitive data/ information	Information of a very personal nature, e.g. medical information
6.1	Spyware	Software that tracks personal information that you type into websites
6.2	Health and Safety	Issues that affect someone's wellbeing when they are using a computer
6.2	Health and Safety Policy	A document that explains the rules relating to Health and Safety
6.2	Physical injury	Caused by an accident when using computers
6.2	Physical strain	Caused by over-use or incorrect use of computers
6.2	RSI (Repetitive strain injury)	Pain that you get when you do the same physical activity over and over again
6.2	Stress	Feeling anxious or under pressure
6.3	Copyright	A law that stops people copying other people's work without permission
6.3	Downloading	Copying something onto your computer - usually from the Internet
6.3	Plagiarism	Copying someone else's work and pretending that you did it
6.3	Research	Finding out information
6.4	Computer technician	Someone who sets up or fixes computers
6.4	Digital divide	Some people have access to computers and some people don't
6.4	Employment	What jobs people do for a living
6.4	ICT access	Whether people can get to use a computer if they want to
6.4	Redundant	When a worker is no longer needed to do their job
6.4	Workplace	Anywhere where people work
6.5	Developed countries	Countries where the people are quite rich
6.5	Developing countries	Countries where people are quite poor but want to get richer
6.5	Newly industrialised countries	Countries that have recently started to develop, e.g. India and China

7.1	Forecast	A prediction of the future based on existing facts
7.1	Keypad	An input device that has numbers or letters on it, e.g. on a cash machine
7.1	Prediction	An estimate of what might happen in the future
7.1	Self-service kiosk	A way of buying things without having to go to a cashier, e.g. a self-service ticket machine
7.1	Stock database	A file that contains information on all of the items owned by a company
7.3	Supercomputer	A computer with large processing power and storage. Used to carry out complex tasks like predicting the weather
7.3	User-interface	What the user of a computer system interacts with (uses) to operate the system
7.3	Visual display	Any device that is used to present information to people

INDEX

Access *see* databases
AgeProof case study   64–7
audio news reports, creating   22–3

bias in information   12–13
Big Brother   95

catalogue shop control system   112–13
CCTV cameras   82, 95
collecting data, methods of   68
computer instructions, writing   84–5, 86, 90–1
computers, using safely   103–5
conditional formatting   63
control systems
    advantages of   93–4
    Big Brother   95
    case study   80–3
    disadvantages of   94
    flowcharts   85, 87, 91
    and monitoring   92–3, 95
    real-life situations   88–9
    repeated instructions   90–1
    writing instructions   84–5, 86, 90–1
copyright   107

data handling
    case study   64–7
    collecting data   68
    integrating with other software   79
    presenting results   76–8
    search techniques   72–5
    structuring data   69
    validating data   69
    see also databases
Data Protection Act   101
databases   68
    datasheet view   65
    design view   65
    forms   70–1
    queries   72–5
    reports   77–8
    setting up   68–9
    software   69
digital divide   108–9
digital photo machines, controlling   84–5
drop-down lists
    database forms   66
    spreadsheets   55

e-portfolios   111
employment, effect of ICT on   108
Excel see spreadsheet models

flowcharts   85, 87, 91
forms
    data collection   68
    database   66, 70–1
    online   71
formulae, spreadsheet   52–3, 55
FrontPage   38–40

graphs, using to model data   56–7

health and safety issues   102
    electrical hazards   103, 104–5
    physical injury   103
    strains, avoiding   102–3
    stress   105
hospital appointment booking system   114–15
HTML (Hypertext Markup Language)
    basic tags   36–7
    creating hyperlinks   37
    simple web page example   32–3
hyperlinks
    buttons as   40, 44
    creating   44–5
    HTML code   37
    in slideshows   19–20
    website structures   42–3

ICT, wider aspects of
    access to ICT   108–9
    across the world   109
    case study   96–9
    effect on employment   108
    health and safety   102–5
    personal data   100–1
identity theft   100
If statements, spreadsheets   55, 63
information
    bias in   12–13
    clarity of   30–1
    finding and presenting case study   4–7
    gathering for news reports   22
    reliability of   9
    up-to-date   13
    validity of   10–11
integrated tasks   110–11
    catalogue shop   112–13
    Choose and Book   114–15
    predicting the weather   116–17

interactive slideshows   20–1
Internet, access to   109
Investment Manager simulation   59–61

keywords, search engines   15, 16

linear website structures   42
links *see* hyperlinks

modelling
    case study   46–9
    creating spreadsheet models   50–3
    and simulations   58–63
    using graphs   56–7
monitoring systems   92–3
    Big Brother   95

navigation on web pages   29–30, 37, 40, 42–5
news reporting   22–3

pedestrian crossing lights, controlling   86–7, 88–9
personal data
    legislation   101
    misuse of   100
    protecting   101
plagiarism   106–7
Popper Party Planners case study   24–7
Powerpoint presentations *see*
    predictions *see* modelling

querying a database   72–5

random numbers, generating   62
random website structures   43
repetitive strain injury (RSI)   103
reports, database   67, 77–8
rules
    flight simulator   59
    spreadsheet models   52–3
    validation   69

safety issues *see* health and safety issues
satellite navigation systems   80–1
search engines   14
    how they work   15–16
    sponsored links   17
    using to check validity   10–11
searching a database   72–5
simulations   58

creating   62–3
Investment Manager   59–61
random number generation   62
variables and rules   58–9
slideshows   18–19
adding hyperlinks   19–20
creating interactive   20–1
software
database   65–7, 69
sound recording   23
spreadsheet   46–63
software for creating web pages
HTML   32–3, 36–7
Microsoft FrontPage   38–40
specialised software   34–5, 38–41
standard software   34
speed cameras   82
spreadsheet models
creating   50–3
developing to improve accuracy
54–5
Investment Manager simulation
59–61
using graphs to model data   56–7
stress, avoiding   105
structure of websites   42–5
styles for web pages   39
swipe cards   82–3

themes for web pages   39

tree website structures   42–3

validating data   69
validity, checking   10–11
variables   52, 58–9

weather forecasting   116–17
web design and creation
case study   24–7
reviewing design   28–31
software for creating   32–41
structuring websites   42–5
websites
checking validity of   10–11
consitent styles/themes   39
creating   32–41
design of   28–31, 42–5
facts versus opinions   9
finding information from   5
navigation   29–30, 37, 40, 42–5
ownership of   8
search engines   10–11, 14–17
structuring   42–5
trusting information on   9
Wizards, FrontPage   40
work stress   105

Yellow Belly Diner case study   46–9